THE BETTING EDGE

THE BETTING EDGE

DAVID-LEE PRIEST

Raceform

About the author

In his fourth book on betting and horse racing, Dr David-Lee Priest sets out to arm punters with a sweeping analysis of profitable systems and approaches. *The Betting Edge* is a gambling manifesto packed with intelligent and thoroughly-researched solutions to the crossword puzzle of finding winners. Priest has served both as a horseracing trader for a spread betting firm and as a racing correspondent for a regional newspaper. His sport psychology research has resulted in a string of academic papers, magazine articles and media interviews including an appearance on the BBC's Breakfast Show in August 2010.

See you in the clubhouse, Unc

Robert William Holland 21.12.1937 – 18.08.2010

Published in 2011 by Raceform
Compton, Newbury, Berkshire, RG20 6NL

Copyright © David-Lee Priest 2011

The right of David-Lee Priest to be identified as the author of this work has
been asserted by him in accordance with the Copyright, Designs and Patents
Act 1988.

A catalogue record for this book is available from the British Library.

ISBN 978-1-906820-86-2

Cover designed by Sarah Chubb
Interiors designed by Fiona Pike

Printed and bound in Great Britain by the MPG Books Group

Contents

*"To each is given a bag of tools,
the shapeless mass, and a book of rules"*
The Heptones

Introduction

Welcome to *The Betting Edge*. If you have encountered my work before then you will already know that I am a miner of sorts. I sink a shaft deep into the dark rock of betting data, work my way along the gallery to the coalface, and mine for profit. Once back at the pit head I sort through the profit ore, discard the ash and polish up the good stuff; a lot of which has found its way onto these pages.

I want to thank the readers who have written to me with their comments and suggestions. When I began the *Against The Odds* series, my intention was to cover the subject matter of betting on horses from every angle. I maintained that making selections could not be separated from betting strategy and the psychology which underpins the whole endeavour. While this remains my view, I have decided to specialise, with the result that the book you are reading is simpler and more focussed than its forbears. **In short, I have written about WHAT to bet on, not HOW to bet or WHY we bet**, which are subjects that deserve a book in their own right. Neither is this a gambling memoir; I won't be wheeling out a string of anecdotes about drunken racing personalities, conspicuous consumption, and hilarious capers in Gloucestershire hotels. Everything in this book is geared towards profit.

From letters and reviews, I have learned that my readership to date is divided into two main groups: serious analytic gamblers and those who are new to betting and perhaps racing also. For this reason, I have written the book in three parts. The first of these covers a trio of essential subjects: an overview of how to make money from betting, a discussion of how to use the betting market to our advantage, and a brief guide to using simple statistics in our search for profit. Part 2 introduces and fleshes out the variables which have some bearing on profit, some of which relate to the horse itself, others to the racecourse. The third and final part consists of an analysis of profitable trends and systems, which is the beating heart of the book. As such, readers of *Against The Odds* who know their racing onions very well are invited to skip Part 2 and head straight for the nitty gritty.

I trust you will enjoy reading this book and take some useful information away from it. Have a great betting year, and be lucky.

David-Lee Priest
Norfolk, 30 August 2011

Acknowledgements:
I would like to thank Julian Brown at the *Racing Post* for his patience and support, my friends and family for their encouragement (mum, dad, Lydia, and Sarah), and Sam Walker and Dave Bellingham, also at the *Racing Post*, for their thoughtful advice. Last but not least I would like to thank Darren Clarke for his helpful comments on the manuscript.

Part 1: Betting Fundamentals

What is the point of a book about betting?

Reviews of such books often open brightly with the expectation that the book's author might spill the beans. However, they inexorably close with the acceptance that he was never really going to. This acceptance is often rationalised with the logic that, if he makes money, then it is not in his interests to give away his secrets. Here we touch on the biggest fundamental truth about betting: **It is like a bucket of crabs**. If one escapee approaches the rim then it will be hauled back into the abyss by the despairing claws of the less profitable. The concept of a betting exchange brings this principle into sharper relief: if I win you lose, so if you lose then I win. It's what evolutionary psychologists refer to as a zero-sum game. There are many theatres in life where people could achieve more if they worked in collaboration; sadly, betting is not one of them.

By definition, any approach that becomes widespread will fail. Conversely, the most exclusive strategies will prove the most successful. This has never been truer than it is today; with the advent of web-based betting forums and improved communication technology, punters are connected as never before. Knowledge is exchanged like wildfire and those highest up the pecking order in each forum pool their knowledge by sharing information about products and services they have subscribed to.

There is a cast iron relationship between profit and secrecy, not because popular selections *perform* any worse but because any weight of money crushes the odds available, especially when it is coming from a group of individuals who appear to be operating in unison. Bookmakers are punters too and they want to stay alive financially by controlling their liabilities. Anyone who experiences annoyance when they are limited or refused by a bookmaker simply doesn't understand the field they are working in. It's like heading out in the rain without an umbrella and moaning that you got wet. If the bookies laid any bet then they would all go broke and there would be nobody to bet with. This principle is the one which is currently threatening to bring *Betfair* to its knees.

We have arrived at what, in my opinion, is the second fundamental truth of betting: **Profit is a fragile and transient creature and its most fearsome predator is publicity**. A memorable demonstration of this principle was provided by Nick Mordin in his book *Winning Without Thinking* (Aesculus Press, 2006). He scoured the formbook comments of race-readers for animals that had won well, before dividing his sample into two groups: Those winners who were described in glowing terms such as "easily" or "impressively" and a second group whose stellar performances only became clear by looking at the comment pertaining to the second-placed horse (such as "no chance with winner"). The "obvious" winners in the former group did not prove profitable to follow in their subsequent starts whereas the better-concealed ones did. Such is the way of things. Incidentally, Mordin comes highly recommended.

The jealous and insecure in the gambling fraternity, in other words most of us, delight in declaring that a notable gambler (particularly one who has won minor celebrity) is now "washed up" and has "lost it" – that he has fallen back into the bucket as it were. However, I don't think that will ever be true with Nick Mordin. There might be people who make more money, but there are none who can communicate their profit instinct as well as he does. I have never met or communicated with him, but I am sure he will always do well – because a man with those tools should always be rich.

An "impressive" winner of the sort Nick Mordin identifies:
Frankel winning the 2,000 Guineas in 2011

So surely I will keep all the juicy information to myself, and all that this book will amount to is "crumbs from the table". To build on the food analogy, you might suspect that I have invited you round for afternoon tea but that all I am going to bring out is a plate of digestives, keeping the chocolate-chip cookies entirely for myself! Well you'd be wrong in that. Yes, there are some digestives on the plate – there is a place for them – but you will also find a cookie or two to dunk in the tea of your own betting wisdom, and I don't begrudge you these. More importantly, I am going to tell you about the recipes I use. Some people like to *buy* the cookies you see, and so become dependent on the seller. But I think it preferable to make one's own. And that's a very serious point, albeit frivolously made: The real goal is to be able to develop your own betting methodology, not simply lean on another gambler's ideas. The actual systems and selections are **entirely expendable**.

Alas, there are quite a few people who buy betting books and are dismayed to find that the author, and I quote, "only shows what has worked in the past". They are indignant that he has not provided a neat list of selections to back for guaranteed profit over the year to come. It reminds me of Louis Armstrong's quote about the enigma of jazz: "if you have to ask what it is, you'll never know". Some people just don't (and may never) get it, and in a sense they deserve to lose their money. That's okay because it creates an environment where you and I can make some profit, and that's what this whole thing is about. **Let's not pontificate here. This isn't a hobby or a pasttime. I am here to win money. That attitude is the seed of success. I'm not saying that if you feel that way you'll definitely win, but if you don't feel that way, you'll definitely lose.**

So does that mean none of the trends I write about will be profitable in the future? Not so. When I look back at my previous writings, some of the quirkier ideas that I happened upon were loss-makers the season after the relevant book was published but *many were not*. I have written about these enduring trends several times and yet they seem to weather the betting storms and remain steadfast and unbowed. I will draw attention to these "mighty oaks" as we encounter them. Strangely enough, the systems that I drew especial attention to, perhaps by including them in a summary, appear to be precisely the ones that are now defunct. So I am sure you will understand if I don't include a summary!

Time itself is also a predator of profits. The patterns we uncover in betting data are fluid and will inevitably shift: breeding practices, the alteration of racecourse furniture, the way in which markets are formed, and the *modi operandi* of trainers are ever changing. Yet these fluctuations also create opportunity. For instance, the pioneers who first realised the importance of the draw, and in particular, how it was not accounted for in the *Tricast* formula, made profane amounts of money for a brief spell. Such quantum leaps are rare, but we can always try to look at existing variables in new ways and ask novel questions of the data.

Betting performance is like many other pursuits in that success depends entirely on your performance *relative* to that of others. For this reason, your success is not entirely under your own control. If we accept the apocryphal statistic that 2% of gamblers are consistently in profit, then we have to work harder and smarter than 98% of the betting population in order to become the apex predators in the food chain. It may even be an example of the Pareto principle – 2% of the gamblers making 98% of the profit.

The advent of computer and communications technology has opened a lot of doors and there is now a far greater number of punters out there who are both shrewd and industrious IN THE EXTREME. In order to join them and then remain in their company, it stands to reason that you will have to work *just as hard* and box *just as clever.* That is what I mean when I say that success is relative. One consequence of this state of affairs is that there are thousands of people who have the *knowledge* to make a substantial profit from betting but who simply do not make the effort to do so.

There are approximately three million *Betfair* account holders. Let us use that as a coarse estimate for the number of traders actively involved in the GB market (those who don't play racing markets perhaps being offset by those who bet on horses but not through *Betfair*). Now that leaves us with a fantasy figure of 60,000 souls in annual profit. I suspect the number of bettors who earn the equivalent of a working wage would be FAR fewer, but I digress. This figure of 60k represents a crude headcount of "shrewdies" – those who *know* what they are doing. To back this up with a soft anecdote, I recently encountered one such man on a betting forum who happened to live on my street. Not just in my provincial town but on my very **street**! Now, these individuals are much more likely to pore over betting literature than the typical mug punter. The circulation of this book is likely to amount to some 5,000 copies. So it is conceivable, and not entirely impossible, that EVERYONE reading this can become part of the two-percent-club if they're not already.

As a kid I played in my school basketball team and, contrary to what you'd expect, quite a few of the best players were short. At that level, it was more important that you had a talent for dribbling and shooting because not everyone else did. However, when we look at professional leagues, every player has skill and talent so height does matter. In betting, the ability to select the "right" horses is like the skill in my basketball analogy. It is fundamental – not enough on its own but you can't succeed without it: you wouldn't get to play basketball professionally simply by virtue of being tall but you wouldn't get to play without being tall. So that's what *The Betting Edge* is all about, the simple fundamentals of making profitable selections.

How do I profit?
Let me count the ways

This is my road map of the betting terrain. Each pathway to profit has its own approach and outlook:

1) **Making rule-based selections.** This is when we select runners which fulfil certain criteria. These criteria may relate to the horse (such as *speed rating* or *age*) or the race itself (such as *race distance* or *going*). We may, for example, choose to back topweights on firm ground.

2) **Using ratings.** In this case we assess the performance of an animal according to a numerical scale by which it can be compared with others, an example being the official handicap maintained by the British Horseracing Authority.

3) **Developing mathematical models.** This entails developing a mathematical description of profit using a set of variables which relate to either the race or the horse itself. Typically, a set of equations is used to describe these relationships. Models can vary dramatically in their complexity, from simple approaches such as the assignation of points to each runner, to intricate systems that involve vast networks of algorithms.

4) **Using expertise.** This is the archetypal form of betting which involves forming a subjective decision based on our own assessments of the available information. It is the most complex and powerful method but also the least transparent.

5) **Using inside information.** This is the approach of an individual or group who are able to influence the preparation and running of a horse and who bet with information that is not publically available.

6) **Trading.** This is a method which aims to generate a profit from the movement of prices in the market or the disparity between different bookmakers' odds and their betting products. Hence, no formal knowledge of the event itself is required.

Of course almost all betting approaches are hybrid: For example, **traders** may have an **expert knowledge** of events. Meanwhile, what the **expert** does is essentially an organic process that must, on some level, incorporate **rules** and a form of **mathematical modelling** beyond the power of computers. In order to interpret and make use of the output from **mathematical models** and **ratings**, **rule-based** selection criteria are almost always invoked. Finally, **human expertise** plays a role in every other approach; we are given to interpreting the output of **models** and **ratings**.

In the parlance of betting, the word *system* is synonymous with rule-based selections. Systematic betting is the bedrock of all objective approaches and therefore the mainstay of this book. In fact, every book on betting is essentially about rule-based selections. By way of example, there is not much point discussing ratings if we don't consider how we're going to use them, even if that simply means backing the top-rated horse in the race. Books about the approaches of experts are an attempt to describe the indescribable, so the experts in question often resort to distilling their seasoned wisdom into ... you've guessed it ... a series of rules. But that's not possible, you can't take everything learned over a lifetime of betting at the sharp end and turn it into a simple abstract formula for others to copy. There's no way to circumvent the learning experience itself; the rules and principles only make sense if you have acquired the wisdom to use them. If it was that easy to absorb then everyone would turn pro in their first year. *Education is what remains when you have forgotten everything you've been taught*, as Sir George Savile put it.

Clearly, there are no manuals on the subject of insider gambling and, when we come to trading, the reading matter that abounds also tends to take a rule-based approach to the application of various strategies. For example, we might be guided to search the formbook for animals that take an early lead and then lay these in-running because their odds will drift like barges when they start dropping back through the field.

"You don't want a pie in the sky, when you die, you want something on the ground, while you're around".

Books about mathematical models of prediction are thin on the ground and for good reason, there isn't a mass market for them. The ones that do exist are esoteric and tedious in the extreme as they serve little purpose to the vast majority of bettors who don't want a "pie in the sky" but a sure thing on the ground, while they're around, as Muhammad Ali once said. When it comes to mathematical modelling in horseracing, the devil is in the detail and that detail is commercially sensitive. By far the best place to learn about genetic algorithms or neural networks is in the many books and online tutorials on those subjects. If you have the specific type of intelligence needed to grasp the details involved then applying them to horseracing will be the easy part.

So, while rule-based systems may be seen as outmoded and peripheral by some sections of the betting community, they are in fact wonderfully useful, both as a window into the betting world and as the common denominator of other approaches. They inform the development of mathematical models, shape the strategies of experts, and provide an essential edge for traders. Rule-based systems are the ideal tool for contemplating the variables that we consider when we are analysing a race and considering how these variables might interact.

*"Rules are for the guidance of wise men,
and the obedience of fools"*

Douglas Bader

Building systems

Granted, the systems and approaches I am going to present are of a simple nature. Yet we still need to be aware of some guiding statistical principles if we are to correctly interpret the results.

Sample size and the law of large numbers

Simply put, if we toss a coin ten times then it would be no surprise to get a result like seven heads and three tails, but if we repeat the spin 10,000 times then the distribution of results should approach the expected state (in other words, tails and heads would be roughly equal). This tendency is known as the 'law of large numbers' for which Swiss mathematician Jacob Bernoulli offered a proof in the early 18th century. It's a vital principle in particle physics too. For example, the atoms in this book are each charging all over the place in every direction. If, by chance, they were all to move upwards at the same time, which is entirely possible, the book would leap into the air unbidden. But this never happens because of the law of large numbers: there are millions upon millions of atoms so, in effect, they cancel each other out.

The law of large numbers has a fairly obvious bearing on betting: Take the example of favourites. In a given year, 29% of favourites on the flat might win their respective races. However, if we were to divide the data into 50 small samples of 100 races, we could well find that the percentage of winning favourites varies from 23% to 52% across these smaller groups. As a consequence, the profit or loss derived from backing favourites fluctuates wildly between groups.

Two or three individual results can dramatically alter the overall profit yielded in samples as small as 100 runners. The problem grows in proportion to the prices of the runners we back. In the example above we're dealing with favourites with correspondingly short prices. Yet if we were betting on long-shots then it is clear that even a sample of 1,000 runners would be on the skinny side. If we aimed for 10 per cent profit over time then that would amount to £100 if we staked £1 on each of the thousand runners. Just a single 100-1 winner (perhaps by virtue of a freak occurrence or a nerve-jangling photo-finish) would literally double our total profit. If, prior to the final race in our thousand-runner sample, we had broken even so far then a 100-1 winner would make the difference between a 10 per cent return on our investment or showing a small loss. Bookmakers understand this principle only too well and are always striving to make themselves unsusceptible to individual results.

The problem that we have is that many systems and ideas revolve around a very specific type of runner, say for example novices trained by David Pipe running at Newton Abbot. So the sample sizes are, by definition, very small indeed. And to make matters even worse, we have to guard against using too long a sampling period in terms of time. Patterns of results, and their underlying causes, can easily fluctuate on a seasonal basis. In fact, we have two remedies for this problem of small sample sizes: the first is to increase the sample size by making the rule we are using more general and the second is to consider what statisticians call "meaningfulness".

Increasing the sample size

In practice, I frequently discover strong trends based on small sample sizes. On some occasions I feel very strongly – call it a hunch – that the trend is not caused by chance. It may be robust enough that, if I greatly expanded the sample by using more general criteria, it would still apply in spades. The trick lies in considering the underlying cause of the pattern. You may remember in *Against*

The Odds I reported the effects of having an "inside" draw (being closest to the running rail around the turn). Although I noticed some impressive trends at certain racecourses I also noted the sample sizes were too small. Certainly, if I were to have split the samples up into different years (to see if a profit would follow every season) then the samples involved would be ludicrously small.

So I did two things to increase the sample size. Firstly, I included both the horse drawn innermost and the beast in the neighbouring stall. This doubled the sample size. Then I reasoned that the pattern I was looking at, although magnified by the peculiarities of individual tracks, was essentially caused by the geometric advantage of being able to run the shortest distance around the bend and having the running rail for guidance. So I simply used data from every course! It was a move that flew in the face of conventional wisdom which holds that the draw bias is highly track-specific. Yet on this occasion I was proved right; I discovered a consistent profit, year on year, across all racecourses which constituted evidence of my theory.

Meaningfulness (and significance)

When looking at the results of rule-based systems our aim is generally to find out whether a certain variable influences performance and profit. Let us consider the variable of whether a race is a handicap or a stakes race, which for the sake of argument we will call the "race type" variable. We can now ask, for example, whether we lose more money backing favourites in handicaps or stakes races? This is a type of operation that statisticians might call a *difference* test, the aim of which is to find out whether or not we can declare an actual difference in profit between handicap and stakes favourites. Of course, if the two groups of runners produce exactly the same level of profit (or loss) in our sample then most people would probably agree that there was no difference. On the other hand, if we lost all our money backing favourites in handicaps but won every bet in stakes races, most arbiters would suggest that there was a difference caused by the race-type variable. But what of the grey area in between? And what happens if we want to take the results from our small sample and infer what might happen to ALL favourites in EVERY race, in other words the entire "population" of races. That is where statistics come in.

When we measure a difference we need to assess whether it is caused by the variable in question or simply due to the inherent variability attributable to chance. If we were able to use data from every race that has ever or will ever be run, then we would *know* the outcome. In practice we have a limited sample size and we need to ascertain the "**significance**" of that difference. In statistics, the term "significance" means the likelihood that the result is not simply caused by chance. As logic would suggest, the larger the sample size, the more likely it is that the difference is "significant" and our results would generalise across to another sample from the same population. Now, I enclose the word "significant" in quotes because statisticians use this term in a different sense to that which we use in everyday speech. Statistical difference has *nothing* to do with the **size** of the difference. The term used in statistics for the size of the difference is *meaningfulness*.

In truth, to really understand the nature of the difference we have to consider both its significance and its meaningfulness because the two go hand in hand. The larger, or more *meaningful*, the difference is the more *likely* it is to be significant and thus replicable in other samples. What this means is that if we have an absolutely HUGE sample then even a tiny difference between our two groups is going to be declared "significant" but it won't be deemed meaningful. Let's say that we looked at 50,000 races. If we found that by backing favourites in stakes races we won 2p for every pound staked but only 1p in the case of handicap favourites then, because of the large sample size, the difference would almost certainly be deemed "significant" even though it would not be "meaningful". In other words, if we bet on races in a new season (not included in the original sample) then we would likely find that the same difference in profit emerged but that it wouldn't be of much use to us because of its lack of meaningfulness – there would be no reason to follow handicap favourites as opposed to stakes favourites. A more interesting application for us is that, even in a small sample, if the difference in profit is MASSIVE then it still may prove to be significant – in other words we might still want to bet on the trend we have found. So, from a statistical point of view, it is wrong to say that findings which stem from a small sample are of no utility to us – especially when we are stuck with small samples most of the time.

Up until now I have spoken of a simple scenario with only two "levels" of the variable in question – "race type" can either be *handicap* or *stakes*. In practice, we may encounter variables with many levels such as *going* which has at least seven (hard to heavy) and the *month* the race is held, which of course has 12 levels (January to December). In these cases we are looking for a smooth trend which spans several levels. For example, if we were looking at the performance of fillies in each month of the year we might predict that they would win more often in the spring when they are coming into season. We would therefore be looking for a pattern like the one in Figure 1 rather than the one depicted in Figure 2 (see overleaf). The second set of findings should set bells ringing in our heads: why is the trend so abrupt? It seems arbitrary and does not follow the logic of our prediction; on which subject I'll say more a little later.

I have borne these statistical principles in mind when evaluating the results in this book. Indeed, after 15 years you develop an "eye" for meaningfulness and significance. Ultimately, it comes down to your own attitude to risk: how significant and meaningful does a trend have to be before you would start risking your money? In scientific research, very high levels of significance are often called for because lives may depend on the results. For this reason, statistical tests are configured in a very conservative manner so

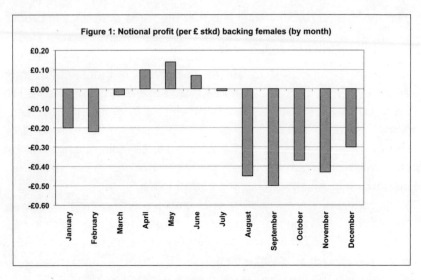

Figure 1: Notional profit (per £ stkd) backing females (by month)

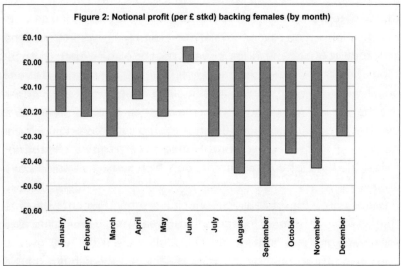

Figure 2: Notional profit (per £ stkd) backing females (by month)

that a hundred guilty men would be freed in preference to hanging one innocent man, as it were. In betting we can of course be a lot more adventurous.

The variability in short-term weather forecasts

Chaos Theory

If we are able to use a large sample of races to test a system, then the chaotic distribution of results is evened out to some extent. Or, to be more precise, the larger the sample, the greater the chance that our results will reflect the underlying trend. I use the word *chaotic* rather than *random* because it is a fallacy to compare complex phenomena like horse races with simple games of chance like roulette or dice. Whereas the latter can reasonably said to be random, the former are determined by a host of complex factors and are essentially subject to the rules of chaos theory. The essence of Chaos Theory is that minute changes to the *starting point* of a system of events ultimately exert **huge** effects on the eventual outcome. It is why meteorologists can predict the weather reasonably well over a short period but when forecasting over a period of more than a week, they stumble. The exact state of the weather at the time of prediction cannot be measured with precise (atomic) accuracy so meteorologists will enter a series of slightly different starting points into their mathematical models. Looking three to four days ahead, the predictions emanating from these different starting points will yield broadly similar weather. For example, there will be small discrepancies of a few miles when we consider the potential position of a certain cold front or cyclone. However, over time the variability in the predictions begins to expand at an exponential rate, so even ten days into the future the algorithms predict wildly different outcomes and the forecasted weather map is a chaotic mess.

I believe that races are a chaotic process and hence the outcomes are far more "uncertain" than it would appear at first glance. If a well-fancied horse wins a race then there is a sense that it was always *going* to win, that the result simply confirmed what most of us already *knew*. This is in fact a psychological illusion. What chaos theory teaches us is that, if we could return in time and run the same race many thousands of times, we would get an infinite variety of different results. Maybe the favourite would still win *most* of them but in an assortment of different ways. In fact, an imperceptible incident when coming out of the stalls might yield a totally different shape to the race. If we then consider the chaotic influence of occurrences that might happen in the weeks or months leading up to the race, then the variety of potential outcomes is truly astronomical. This leads me to suggest a third fundamental truth of betting: **the patterns of results we experience in racing reflect a chaotic process**. What this means is that we always depend on a modicum of good fortune to be successful.

Simplicity

In practice, successful systems tend towards simplicity. The logical principle at stake is called *Occam's Razor* and it states that when predicting a phenomenon, any rules that don't improve the accuracy of the prediction should be stripped away. In other words, if two methods are broadly as effective as each other, then preference is given to the simpler one. I am ever suspicious of prediction models which claim to include every conceivable variable under the sun. No craft we possess is sophisticated enough to do this. Even the highest-functioning neural networks (prediction models that mimic the learning capability of the neurons in the human brain) tend to rely on a small cluster of carefully chosen variables; adding others often impairs the result. The same principle applies when we look at rule-based systems. Clearly, using just one variable (such as the *going*) is too simplistic. In other words, we are not going to make money just by backing every horse running on soft ground. **What we will discover is that the *best performing* and *most reliable* systems generally involve the interaction of two or at the most three variables.**

Interaction

The principle of *interaction* is key to understanding our results. This is where two or more variables interact with each other. Let us return to our analysis of favourites running in handicaps or stakes races. Now if we look at the *actual* results of this analysis as opposed to the hypothetical ones we used in our previous example, we might see that favourites win 30% of the time in stakes races and 24% of the time in handicaps. So do favourites perform better in stakes races than in handicaps? Not necessarily. In fact these results are caused by the interaction with a *third* variable – that of field size (the number of runners in a race). Just to clarify, the first two variables are favouritism (whether a horse is favourite or not) and race-type (handicap or stakes race). Handicaps generally have larger field sizes than stakes races, and of course the more runners, the smaller the percentage chance of victory. This is what statisticians call an *interaction effect* and it is depicted in Figure 3 (see over).

Another kind of relationship between variables that interests us is **correlation**. Consider this hypothetical example, both *favourites* and horses with the *best speed rating in each race* tend to win twice as often as the "average" horse does. So we might conclude that we

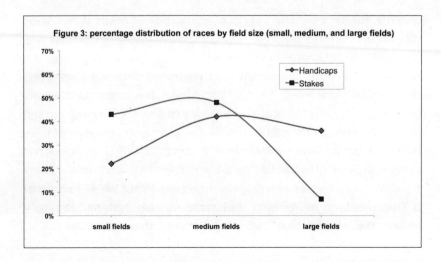

Figure 3: percentage distribution of races by field size (small, medium, and large fields)

should back favourites that are top-rated for speed as these animals would surely win **four times** more often than the average runner. But this is not the case because these two variables are **correlated**, so they are not truly independent of each other. This correlation occurs because if a horse is considered the fastest in the race on speed ratings then it is most likely to be made favourite anyway. If we stack positive factors together in this way then we see a law of diminishing returns.

Back fitting

The most serious error we can commit when building systems is to **back-fit** them, which is the equivalent of putting your trousers on before your pants. Back-fitting is to arbitrarily increase the complexity of a system until it produces a profit when applied to a *specific dataset*. It is a simple truth that the more variables we use, and the more we specify these variables, then the more likely it is that *some combination* of them will yield a profit. But this profit will be an arbitrary profit; merely the product of chance. Back-fitting is the hallmark of systems pedalled by conmen and scammers. A classic example would be a system that specifies a list of racecourses you should consider when following a certain type of selection. This is likely to simply be the courses which showed a profit during the sample in question. By rights, *some combination* of courses will always lead to a profit. All it would take is one big-priced winner during a season and boom! that course is in profit. Naturally, I would be a fool to follow this system because there is no underlying sense behind it. The counter example would be a system with a crystallized logic – for example, backing a certain Newmarket trainer's runners at *all* Scottish tracks because the journey involved meant that he or she wouldn't make the effort if the animal was not primed to win.

The subject of back-fitting is particularly relevant to the use of "filters", which are typically negative rules added to a system such as "don't bet on females" or "don't bet in races with over 12 runners". If you eliminate any categories of races or types of horses then it is imperative that you have a sound reason for doing so. If selections in a particular category yield unfavourable results then this might be due to a statistical aberration. Hence, if your selections perform poorly in August but not in September or July then you should question why this is. Look for smooth trends in the data that reveal an underlying effect rather than arbitrary peaks and troughs which could signify nothing.

Because of the perils of back-fitting I strive, when developing and testing a system, to not pull too many strings in order to force a solution that returns profits. You will have to refine a system to some extent as a matter of course but if you bend over backwards in the attempt then you will find that your method generalises poorly. With this in mind, I tend to treat the data in quite a "rough" manner, reasoning that if my idea holds water then I won't need to precisely tailor my analysis in order to find profit. A stock method to help us avoid back-fitting is to test systems on different datasets. The best tactic is to use the data from different seasons; an approach which is especially fit for our purpose in that we can answer the question:

"What would happen in practice if I ran this system?" While we may accept a losing week or month in the context of annual profit, most gamblers would not countenance a losing year. Another way of avoiding back-fitting is to follow the scientific method.

Scientific method

The analytic approach I favour bears a strong resemblance to the scientific method that I've been trained in: firstly, a hypothesis is formed based on logic, experience, or evidence, or even just a hunch. This hypothesis is usually an idea which can be simply expressed and has its basis in logic – for example "it is profitable to lay topweights on heavy ground because it is harder to carry weight when the ground is slow". The next stage is to design a method of testing this hypothesis using the available data. Finally, one is in the position to accept or reject the hypothesis and ultimately predict what may occur in future races.

"I have not failed 700 times, I have not failed once. I have succeeded in proving those 700 ways will not work. When I have eliminated the ways that will not work, I will find the way that will work"
Thomas Edison

As with all scientific endeavour, it is just as important to know what doesn't work as it is to be aware of what does. There is every reason for me to tell you that a certain approach is disappointing or cannot be mined for profit because then you won't waste time retreading my failed steps. You might even be able to spot a flaw in my reasoning and improve on my method to secure a profit. Only reporting your work when you found what you expected and were therefore "right" is the epitomy of bad science. It is an objective principle I hold to, so I make no apology for including in my report the odd null finding that cannot be turned directly into profit.

"I don't make predictions ... and I never will!"
Des Lynam

The fallacy of prediction

To avoid back-fitting it is essential to specify the hypothesis *in advance* rather than looking at the data and then suggesting an explanation to account for its patterns. This idea is explored thoroughly in Nassim Nicholas Taleb's provocative book *The Black Swan: The Impact of the Highly Improbable* (Penguin, 2011). Using potent examples from empirical work, he explains how humans are almost incapable of accurately predicting future events that arise from complex causes and, even worse, how we engage in a whole battery of self-deceptions by back-fitting a narrative to explain and post-rationalise these events. In Taleb's conception, the worst offenders are the so called "experts" in the fields of social science and economics. These individuals, professors and fund managers in their number, are almost fatally hamstrung by their twin delusions that complex events can be predicted and that they are especially skilled in that direction. This resonated with me as a gambler (and as a disgruntled social scientist) because the essence of success in betting is scepticism and counter-intuition whereas the essence of failure is credulity and following the conventional wisdom of the crowd.

Recently, I have encountered the research of Paul Fletcher, the Bernard Wolfe Professor of Health Neuroscience in the Department of Psychiatry at Cambridge University. Using brain imaging techniques he has discovered that **what** we perceive is often determined by our anticipations and what fits most comfortably with our prior expectations and biases. The everyday experience of taking in data from the world, weighing it up and drawing conclusions implies

An infamous Black Swan

that information flows exclusively in one direction: from perception to belief. Actually, it is a two-way street. It's just that our beliefs about what is normal, predictable or logical may prevent us from experiencing the perceptions that violate our assumptions.

As part of a Channel 4 Special in February 2008, the illusionist Derren Brown managed to convince a woman to invest her life savings in a horse that he tipped. The confidence trick worked because he had sent her a winning tip every week for five weeks. What she didn't know was that she had been one of 7,776 people that Brown had originally started sending advice to. Her willingness to believe in Brown's system just goes to show the degree to which people are willing to believe in a 'system'. Humans are, in essence, pattern recognition machines.

Collectively, what I have learned from philosopher Taleb, neuropsychiatrist Fletcher, and illusionist Brown is that there is no such thing as prediction in the conventional sense. People don't

Derren Brown predicted a small crowd at Wolverhampton

forecast the results of horse races. How many times in your life have you been able to confidently predict the entire finishing order of a race, let alone how the race will pan out? Even the industry's most fêted tipsters and professionals make fairly limited "predictions" which are proved wrong almost all of the time. Yet their crude prescriptions when followed do amount to profit. That doesn't make them seers; it just means they are adept at systematically exploiting weaknesses in the *betting market*. Take the Sussex Stakes of 2011 by way of example, opinion from experts was divided on the outcome of this titanic clash between Frankel and Canford Cliffs. The former's victory seems staggeringly obvious now but a sizeable percentage of those in the industry didn't foresee it, much less the manner of the victory. The only true "experts" are those who can perceive the limitations of their predictive expertise. I would go further, the whole betting industry, and by extension the sport of kings, exists simply because people can't perceive their failings as prognosticators.

Frankel winning the Sussex Stakes

"When you bet it must be a value bet".
Professor Frank George

"The only thing that really matters is the odds."
Old time professional gambler **Morton Coles**

"The greatest of all gifts is the power to estimate things at their true worth"
François de La Rochefoucauld
17th Century French Nobleman

Value

In betting, value is everything and everything is value. Indeed, our lives are built on value. We place a "value" on ourselves, our time, and the lives of others. In Marxist ideology we find the principle of an "exchange value" placed upon things which people have to offer: job-specific skills in an employment context, for example. I propose that the fourth fundamental truth about betting goes something like this: **What happens on the racetrack only matters** *indirectly.* **What really matters is the prism of the betting market.** The market is a far, far more potent predictor of racehorse performance than any system devised by individual gamblers with their neural networks and ram-laden computers. This is because the market benefits from a process outlined by James Surowiecki in his 2005 book *The Wisdom Of Crowds* (Abacus): namely, the aggregation of information by groups and the resulting superiority of collective decisions over those made by individual members of that group. In a pop-science experiment broadcast as part of the recent BBC series *The Code*, amiable mathematician Marcus Du Sautoy asked 160 people to guess the number of jellybeans in a copious glass jar.

Their individual estimates were wildly inaccurate in both directions, ranging from several hundred to many tens of thousands (the actual number was 4,510). Then Du Sautoy produced his trusty calculator and began calculating the mean average of the predictions. With televisual panache he gasped as the answer popped up: 4,514.90 beans – just 4.90 beans out. Something similar is happening in the betting market which, via the machinations of *Oddschecker* and *Betfair*, has become like some sort of vast collective unconscious.

The mathematician Marcus du Sautoy

When it comes to predicting racing performance, the general superiority of the betting market over the methods of individuals isn't hard to fathom. Even a suite of the most advanced neural networks operated by an expert accounts for a limited number of variables and has far less computational power than a single human brain, let alone three million brains. The attempt to develop a system which outperforms the betting market *across the board* in its predictions of racehorse performance is a holy grail for the mathematically minded. I would assess the chances for success as being broadly in line with those of the zealots who quested for the actual cup of Christ. What such systems do achieve is to identify very minimal inefficiencies in the market which can be exploited for profit (which is not the same thing as "outperforming" the market).

Trying to outperform the betting market

It is important to bear in mind that, while the betting market is a good predictor of performance, it is in no way a literal representation of each animal's "chances" of victory. Horse races are so intrinsically chaotic that any attempt to accurately predict the true probabilities is almost certainly futile. Rather than a literal assessment of probability, the market is a model of the collective views of the betting public. Frequently, the prices on offer say more about the punting masses, their prejudices, and their antagonistic relationship with bookmakers than they do about the horses in the race. **Even so,**

the market is our theatre of operations. So our focus switches from "what is going to win?" to "what is going to win me money?" This perspective compels us to take a long-term view. If we want to win money in a single race then the right horse to back is nearly always the favourite. If we want to win money over a season then the right horse to back is never the favourite. We are dealing with animals which are **undervalued** by the betting market and which will, due to the law of large numbers, make up to a profit over many bets.

In fact, the law of large numbers tells us that, the longer we bet for, the more likely we are to be in profit (assuming nothing changes to reduce the profitability of our selections). Let's say we are backing a horse at 8/1 that we feel has been undervalued. While impossible to know the *true* odds, let us place a notional value on them of 5/1. In this example we are virtually *guaranteed* to make money in the long term if we make identical selections. Yet our prospects of success in *this race* are slim, around 17%. This has brought us to my fifth fundamental truth of betting – **to win we must take a long-term view**.

What is value then?

By now we have prepared the ground sufficiently to permit a definition of value: **value is a series of bets in profit**. In other words, if we have made a profit over time then our bets represented value, if we haven't then they didn't. What I am saying is that value can only be assessed retrospectively and only in the long term. We might *feel* an individual bet is "value" because it will eventually form part of a series of profitable bets, but we will only know with *hindsight* whether or not we have beaten the market over time. Nevertheless, our assessment of potential value on a bet-by-bet basis is what leads us to that long-term profit. Perceived value is entirely a matter of perspective. For example, you approach racing from a pedigree angle then you will esteem value in a bet that a speed-ratings expert will not.

The question in your head should be: **at what price would I back this horse?** Let's say there were 3/1 joint favourites in a race and I was sweet on one of them. If you asked me whether I'd back the other one, my answer would probably be "no". You might persist and say, "what about if I offered you 4/1?". Now I would have a decision to make, but the answer would still be no. Then you might up the ante: "what if I offered you 6s?" If I refused your new offer I'd be an idiot. But that's how many punters think – they wouldn't want to be on the "other one" at any price. The principle at stake is this one: if you were short of cash and I said "do you wanna buy a new Mercedes?" you'd tell me to jog on, and then jog on some more. But if I said "you can have it for a grand in the hand", you'd probably rip my arm off whether you were broke or not. That's value.

How to obtain value?

Profitable systems generally identify favourably priced runners that are overlooked by the betting public. Hence, part of the logic to such systems is that they select horses which appear to be poor bets from a conventional point of view. As the odds that you will be able to obtain about a selection depend on the betting public's opinion, backing fancied horses will drastically reduce your ability to show a profit. Contrastingly, if you can lay horses that are given too much respect by the punting masses then you might profit from their collective misapprehensions. What this means is that profitable systems are never simply about conventional selection criteria such as form or ratings, but the ways in which that information is processed by other gamblers.

If you think your system is built around speed – it isn't – it's built around limitations or flaws in others' knowledge of speed. If you think your system is built around pedigrees – it isn't – it's built around limitations or flaws in others' knowledge of pedigrees. That's another feature of the systems pedalled by shysters and conmen – they're just a stack of obvious criteria: back last-time-out winners, returning to the racecourse after less than 30 days, at single figure odds, trained by a handler with a winning record at the racecourse in question, placed on the same going before ... That's just like bringing sand to the beach.

An interesting property of the betting market is its reflexivity, which in the mathematical sense means that it influences itself. What I am trying to say is that punters form judgements about runners based solely on the price, so people support hot favs simply because they're hot favs – even before they have looked at the horse's credentials. At the other end of the scale, there are gamblers who back an outsider because it will provide them with a big return if it wins. This partly explains the common misnomer that "value" refers merely to the size of the price on offer. We hear racing commentators routinely observing that any given horse with odds above 10-1 has a "value price". In short, there is a whole generation of people working in the racing media who have confused the concept of value with that of outsiders.

Should we forget about winners in our search for value? I will confess my take used to mirror the stock view expressed by Barry Meadow in *Money Secrets at the Racetrack* (1990, TR Publishing), namely that the right approach is somewhere in between value and winners. I have revised my opinion and I would now say the right approach is value *anchored* by winners. What this means in practice is to refrain from *exclusively* backing longshots because of the uncertain rate of return which ensues (even when value has been taken into account).

Direct and Indirect value

A natural consequence of basing our selections on value is that we have to fully consider the other runners in the race. Because of the market mechanism, the price we obtain about our selection will be partly determined by the betting activity relating to those other runners, particularly the beasts that head the market. Hence, we may well have obtained value because other runners were overvalued, not because our fancy was *systematically* undervalued. To help attune myself to this concept I gave names to these two different types of value. I called the undervaluing of a horse by the market *direct value*, whereas the achievement of a favourable price predominantly because of the over-valuing of a market leader I termed *indirect value*. Direct value comes about when there is a *systematic reason* for the runner to represent better value. In turn, this precipitates an overvaluation of other animals in the race. In the case of *indirect value*, it is the overvaluation of another runner or group of runners which creates the value in our selection. Typically, rule-based systems of the type I will present in Part 3 work on a simple level: they churn out selections which represent direct value. It stands to reason that direct value is greater than indirect value, and that the greatest value of all occurs when there is both *direct* and *indirect* value. Both types of value would coincide when there is a market leader that we could oppose in its own right running in the same race as a less-fancied runner that we are seeking to back for a systematic reason.

The Market

Starting prices (SPs)

The formula by which SPs are determined changed in November 2006. Previously, SPs were determined from a sample of on-course bookmakers' prices at the off: specifically, the lowest price among the best third available to "good money". Following the change, the SP is now the lowest price among the best 50 per cent, which includes the bookmakers betting each way in the case of quieter meetings. There is also a provision for greater input from the on-course representatives of major betting-shop chains.

Changes in SP percentages

For those unfamiliar with the concept of SP percentages, I have provided this information at the end of the book. Prior to the 2006 regulatory changes in the SP formula, the SP percentage per runner was dropping year on year, from a high of 2.07% in September 2000 to 1.45% in September 2006. This depreciation was largely due to the influence of the *Betfair* market and the hedging activity that it created, coupled with the competition fostered by odds-comparison websites. Post-2006, the margin crept back up to its former 2% level, which caused some degree of controversy, before rebounding back down towards the 1.8% level at which it resides in the summer of 2011.

The efficiency of the betting market

This analysis, displayed in Figure 4, shows us the return derived from backing every National Hunt runner in the UK over the past three years. It provides us with a baseline against which to compare all system results. The two lines in the figure represent the strike rate percentage of runners and the returns derived from backing them, which appear in the standard metric of profit / loss per £1 staked.

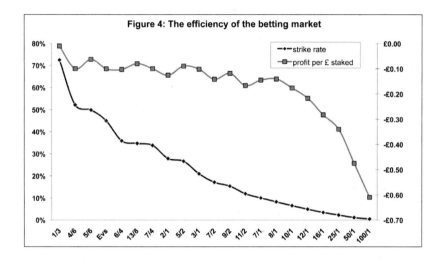

Figure 4: The efficiency of the betting market

As we can see, backing horses that started heavily odds-on came within a whisker of generating profit, whereas the less-fancied runners produced an abysmal rate of return if backed blindly. The same type of analysis has been undertaken by many academic researchers in the past two decades. The results are typically very similar and the prevailing trend is now referred to as the "favourite-longshot bias". Many strange reasons have been advanced to explain why longer-priced horses offer a much lower return than favourites. I favour the explanation that bookmakers must achieve their over-round percentage in some manner. If the return derived from backing market leaders was very poor then the lack of value would appear obvious to backers. It is less noticeable to offer unfair odds about the runners that few backers will be supporting as opposed to the favoured horses that are driving the market. Furthermore, bookmakers are forced to compete to a greater extent in order to attract money for runners at the business end of the market. Notably, the favourite-longshot bias has softened considerably over recent years, to the extent that runners priced in single figures are now broadly equivalent in terms of the return derived from backing them. This is doubtless a product of a more competitive market which has increased efficiency.

Understandably, the SP percentage affects the return we can expect about a runner in any price bracket. However, the biggest advantage of a low SP percentage is felt when backing horses at the higher odds. It's tempting to think that if we can achieve a better SP percentage then the runner we aim to back will be available at a longer price. In practice, the business end of the market is highly competitive and, when it comes to horses trading in single figures, we may not get an advantage by utilising markets with a lower SP percentage.

SP filtering

When running systems, we can use forecasted odds as an efficient way of narrowing down a field. One such approach is to dismiss any runner whose price falls above the number of runners in a race – 16/1 being the upper bound in a race of 16 runners, for example. Historically, 80-85 per cent of races are won by horses that meet this criterion.

Prices and betting strategy

What prices should we bet at? What we can surmise straight away is that, in the case of industry SPs, backing a winner from the runners which go off at 33/1+ is like trying to find a white mouse in a snowstorm. Added to this is the fact that many of these winners will have benefitted from freak occurrences that reflect the chaotic nature of the sport. On the plus side, there is a possibility of attaining much greater value when backing outsiders. It's just that these opportunities are few and far between; very rare birds indeed. We have already established that horses at the short end of the market are unlikely to represent value. Again, we have to consider the inherent chaos of results. In simple terms, every horse is susceptible to what Dr. Peter May referred to as the "accident factor", regardless of its price. A worrying host of ailments and misfortunes can afflict any horse without warning. For example, in chases, eight per cent of odds-on favourites fall, unseat their riders, or refuse to jump.

So it follows that the sixth fundamental truth about betting is this: **in between the short prices and the long-shots there is a band which represents our greatest chance of reliable profits when backing**; a notion I have illustrated in Figure 5.

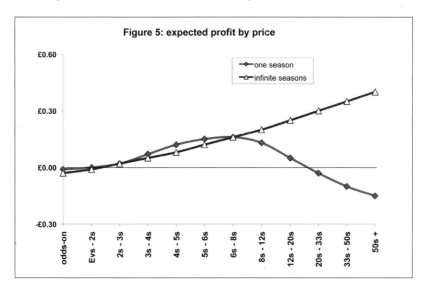

What cements this fundamental truth is the chaotic mathematics of losing runs. Let us say we have a system that is churning out selections which we are able to back at an average price of 5/1. Now let's say these beasts win 20 per cent of the time. According to the law of large numbers, our profit over time should be 20p for every £1 staked. We might be forgiven for presuming that our accumulation of profits should be fairly constant. Nothing could be further from the truth. Even in this ordered example, computer simulations demonstrate that losing runs of twenty or more bets would be commonplace. Already we would need a pretty strong backbone. If our stakes were £100 then we'd have to be quite content to witness £2,000 depart from our account with no guarantees that the forthcoming results would even out the trend *in the short term*.

The belief that a series of independent events is connected has been dubbed the "gambler's fallacy". It's the notion that, if heads has come up ten times on the spin, tails must be "due"; a straightforward misinterpretation of the law of large numbers. It is the gambler's fallacy that leads us to underestimate the likelihood of long losing runs. If the variability we face at shorter odds is considerable, imagine the situation at 33/1. Vast deserts of losers with the occasional winning oasis, and plenty of mirages to boot.

While "dutching" multiple outsiders in a race may feel like a very neat solution to the problem of losing runs, it is unlikely that *several* runners would simultaneously represent value. When this does happen it is typically because a favourite is *massively* over-valued. The times when dutching is advantageous are outnumbered by instances in which we simply want to back an undervalued runner or lay an overvalued one.

When I began writing about betting, I championed the 4/1-8/1 bracket which I felt was key to my success as that is where my profits lay. However, since the actual "band" of prices you work with is not so important, it doesn't even need to be constant. What's important is the principle at stake, which is essentially a compromise between two imperatives: avoiding horses that have been overvalued by the betting public while maximising the probability of making a **consistent** profit. This principle characterises the modus operandi of almost every successful gambler I've met or read about – in this country and abroad – that's why I regard it as a universal.

Laying

In this book, I present ideas for profit based around laying as well as backing. I used to think that one had to have a layer's mentality because punters seem to gravitate to one discipline or the other.

While this may be true in practice, the inclination to either lay or back is a matter of behaviour rather than knowledge. In fact, when talking about making profit from a race I don't think the concepts of backing and laying can be meaningfully separated. To understand one you must understand the other; they are flip sides of the profit coin. Also, the distinction between them is somewhat illusory: in a six-horse race, if you back three of them, you've laid the others! Just as we find with backing systems, the laying systems that don't work are the ones which feature a compendium of all the "obvious" criteria: trainer out of form, stepping up in class, unplaced last time out, etc.

There is certainly no wholesale advantage to be had from laying as opposed to backing. Punters who are still living in the nineties might feel that laying is a magic wand. After all, "it's easier to find losers than winners" and "they call the bookies layers don't they?" But the markets are too efficient for that to be the case. In fact, the activity of layers has shaped the market. The fear of laying big prices has probably contributed to a softening of the favourite-longshot bias over the past ten years. In other words, I feel runners going off at single-figure odds present more value than they used to because of the activity of layers, many of whom operate a ceiling price above which they won't lay.

When it comes to horses at bigger prices, the "fairness" of the *Betfair* market in comparison with the bookmakers' offerings often works to the severe detriment of layers. Not only can you not bet much but the prices that represent value to backers are anything but for layers. How would you feel if you'd offered 116.5 about *Big Dano*, who returned 28/1 with the industry on 17 May 2011? It is mighty clear who got the "value" there. So the attitude of the layer is often a hyper-conservative one. It is worth noting that *Betfair* customers who tried to "buy" money at odds of 0.01 (100/1 on) were reportedly £200,000 down in one year (from *Game, Set and Matched* by Iain Fletcher). There is even a website (gubbage.com)

A horse getting pipped on the line

dedicated to 1/100 losers on *Betfair*, and the videos of their mishaps make entertaining viewing (if you didn't back them yourself!).

Part 2: The Variables

The pages that follow introduce the variables that we might use in selection systems and discuss the issues around them.

Specialisms

The subdivisions in racing are like sports within a sport and it will always prove more profitable to specialise. The trick is to know that certain variables are of more relevance in some domains of racing than in others. For example, if you hone in on races for two-year-olds then speed ratings and the trainer's strike rate would probably be the most important considerations.

The races that comprise the annual fixture list are not a nebulous mass. Rather, racing is divided into discrete domains that can be thought of as separate. The following statement is virtually a consensus among the successful backers that I have encountered: betting in each category of racing has its own considerations and consequently each requires a special approach. Hence, many of the analyses in Part 3 will be focussed on specific types of races. In the following list, I will briefly introduce the distinctions that I draw:

- **CODE:** TURF (Flat)/ALL-WEATHER (Flat)/NATIONAL HUNT (Jumps)
  Flat racing and jump racing are quite rightly regarded as different sports. Likewise, all-weather flat racing is an entirely separate arena to its turf counterpart. The artificial surfaces produce different patterns of results when compared to the turf. Generally, the ability that horses demonstrate on one surface does not translate well to the other. When I refer to 'flat' races I will be writing about those run on turf. If I want to indicate all-weather races then I will do this explicitly.

An All-Weather race

• OBSTACLES IN NATIONAL HUNT RACES

Horses that run under National Hunt rules often begin their careers by competing in National Hunt flat races, otherwise known as "bumpers". This practice provides younger horses which have not graduated from flat racing with an opportunity to develop their racing skills and fitness levels prior to their first run over obstacles. Hence, bumpers are regarded as distinct from other National Hunt races and I have not included them in the majority of analyses that relate to jump racing as they distort the results of the tests. There is a qualitative difference between the two different types of obstacles that are used in jump racing, namely hurdles and fences. The fences used in steeplechasing present a far more rigorous jumping proposition not simply because of their height but also by virtue of their rigidity. For this reason, the technique used to jump fences is not merely an extension of that used to clear hurdles. Because of these differences, I have analysed hurdle races and steeplechases separately in some instances.

A hurdle

A fence

- **HANDICAPS AND NON-HANDICAPS**
The significance of this distinction should not be underestimated.
The principle of handicapping horses with saddle-weight
according to their perceived ability results in patterns of
performance which are very distinct from those observed in
non-handicap races. Indeed, handicaps are really a code within a
code. It is more typical for a horse to run predominantly in either
handicaps or non-handicaps than to oscillate between the two.
In fact, some horses become known as "handicappers" due to
their assimilation into this sphere of racing. All horses begin their
careers in non-handicaps and subsequently progress through
maiden or novice races against other less-seasoned opponents. If
a horse shows consistent improvement and relatively high ability
then it will continue to progress along the pattern of ever more
competitive non-handicap races. But most horses eventually
find their way into the handicap fold sooner or later. Indeed,
for the less able, handicaps provide the major opportunity for
competition. The best handicaps of the year are extremely
competitive and include some very able horses; this is especially
so in National Hunt racing, where a high proportion of the fastest
and most valuable races are handicaps.

- **AGE OF HORSES**
In both flat and jumps racing, horses generally begin their
careers with a succession of races in which they compete against
other juveniles. This framework enables younger horses to
mature and race competitively before they acquire the requisite
physical development to challenge their seniors. Juvenile races
often yield distinct trends when analysed. In some instances I
have considered it necessary to examine the performances of
juveniles and older horses separately, or focus purely on mature
horses. In flat racing, a horse is eligible to race from the age of
two. To simplify matters, all horses share an equine birthday

on the first of January. For this reason, no horse turns three during the flat season on the turf, which lasts from late March until early November. Two-year-olds seldom compete with their elders. Hence, it is a simple procedure to identify juvenile races. Flat horses continue to mature markedly after they turn three. However, for the purposes of analysis, I have identified two-year-olds as juveniles. In the case of jump racing, horses may begin competing in juvenile hurdles and bumpers at the tender age of three, although it is equally possible that they enter the National Hunt code from the flat racing domain when they are considerably older.

Power, a leading two-year-old of the 2011 Flat season

- **CONDITIONS OF RACES**
  Besides their status as either handicaps or non-handicaps, races are defined by various eligibility conditions that alter their character. For example, the entrants may be maidens (yet to win a race), novices (inexperienced jumpers), or hunter-chasers (National Hunt horses that are licensed to participate in hunting). Some races are only open to horses of one sex. For example, the

Epsom Oaks is contested by three-year-old fillies. After "selling" races, the winning horse is auctioned, whereas in the case of "claiming" races, the weight borne by each runner is determined by the price that its owner is willing to sell the horse for after the race. Thus, the horses that are deemed the most valuable carry the highest weights. There are other more arbitrary conditions that apply to a small number of races. However, the foregoing list encompasses all of the principal variations.

- **THE ABILITY OF HORSES CONTESTING RACES**
Races are graded in terms of the ability of the horses that contest them. Following a report by the British Horseracing Board's racing review committee, the structure of flat racing was markedly changed in September 2004 and then further revised in July 2008. The essential aim of the process was to simplify the classification system and align each division more closely to specific prize money bands. Before the changes, there were wide discrepancies in prize money between races within the same grade. In some instances, races were able to offer higher prize money than that which was available for higher-grade contests. The previous division into eight classes (A-H) has been simplified into seven grades.

    Class 1 is the equivalent of the former Class A, which includes the best races. At the bottom of the scale, **Class 7** is the preserve of the poorest handicappers on the flat, whereas the lowest level of jumps racing is **Class 6**, which contains the national hunt flat and hunter chase races. I have included two tables to display the entire classification scheme. National Hunt racing was afforded a new classification system along similar lines in January 2006. In some instances, the races in these various strata of ability are subject to different trends, and this is a factor that I have attempted to account for at various junctures.

TABLE 1: CLASSIFICATION OF FLAT RACES

	3-y-o+ 2011	2-y-o+ 2011	
Class 1			
Group 1	£160,000	£130,000	Min Value
Group 2	£80,000	£60,000	Min Value
Group 3	£50,000	£34,000	Min Value
Listed (including those Listed Handicaps 96-110)	£30,000	£21,500	Min Value
Class 2			
Heritage Handicaps	£60,000		Min Value
Handicaps 0-105, 0-110 and Open	£27,500		Min Value
Conditions Stakes			
Handicaps 86-100, 91-105 and 96-110			
Nursery Handicaps – Open			
Classified Stakes 0-95			
Novices and Maidens	£12,500	£9,400	Min Value
Class 3			
Conditions Stakes			
Handicaps 76-90 and 81-95			
Classified Stakes 0-85 to 0-90			
Nursery Handicaps 0-90 and 0-95			
Novices and Maidens			
Class 4			
Handicaps 66-80 and 71-85			
Classified Stakes 0-80			
Nursery Handicaps 0-80 and 0-85			
Novices/Novice Auction/Novice Median Auction			
Maidens/Maiden Auction/Median Auction Maiden			
Claiming and Selling Races			
Class 5			
Handicaps 56-70 and 61-75			
Nursery Handicaps and Classified Stakes 0-70 to 0-75			
Novices/Novice Auction/Novice Median Auction			
Maidens/Maiden Auction/Median Auction Maiden/Rating Related Maiden Claiming and Selling Races			

Class 6			
Handicaps 46-60 and 51-65			
Nursery Handicaps and Classified Stakes 0-60 and 0-65			
Novice Auction/Novice Median Auction			
Maiden Auction/Median Auction Maiden/Rating Related Maiden			
Claiming and Selling Races			
Class 7			
Handicaps 45-50			

* All Races Total Prize Fund NB1: No race at Class 3 or below will have prize money of less than £2,250. NB2: all Handicaps of 13.5f and above will have 20lb weight-ranges, i.e. Class 2 will be 86-105 and 81-100, Class 3 76-95 and 71-90 etc, at all times. NB3: all Handicaps will have 20lb weight-ranges during the months of June, July and August.

TABLE 2: CLASSIFICATION OF JUMPS RACES

Classes:	Steeple Chases 2011	Novices Steeple Chases 2011	Hurdles 2011	Hurdles and Juvenile Hurdles 2011	National Hunt Flat Races 2011	
Class 1						
Grade 1	£74,000	£36,500	£56,000	£29,500	£17,800	Min Value
Grade 2	£36,500	£23,400	£29,500	£21,200	£14,800	Min Value
Grade 3	£36,500		£32,500			Min Value
Listed Races	£17,400	£14,200	£15,500	£12,400	£11,000	Min Value
Class 2						
Open Handicaps	£15,500		£12,800			Min Value
Weight-for-age Conditions Races						
Handicaps 0-140+						
Open Novices Handicaps						
Weight-for-age Novices, Juvenile and Beginners Races						
National Hunt Flat Races						
Hunters Steeple Chases	£12,400		£9,700		£9,700	Min Value
Class 3						
Handicaps & Novices Handicaps 0-120 to 0-135						
Weight-for-age Novices Races 0-120 to 0-135						
Weight-for-age Novices, Beginners, Juvenile and Maiden Races						
National Hunt Flat Races						
Hunters Steeple Chases						
Class 4						
Handicaps and Novices Handicaps						

Classes:	Steeple Chases 2011	Novices Steeple Chases 2011	Hurdles 2011	Hurdles and Juvenile Hurdles 2011	National Hunt Flat Races 2011		
0-100 to 0-115							
Weight-for-age Novices Races 0-110 to 0-115							
Weight-for-age Novices, Beginners, Juvenile and Maiden Races							
Weight-for-age Claiming & Selling Races							
National Hunt Flat Races							
Hunters Steeple Chases							
Class 5							
Handicaps and Novices Handicaps 0-85 to 0-95							
Classified Races 0-85 to 0-95							
Weight-for-age Maiden & Beginners Races							
Weight-for-age Claiming Races, Selling Races and Selling Handicaps							
National Hunt Flat Races							
Hunters Steeple Chases							
Class 6							
National Hunt Flat Races							
Hunters Steeple Chases							

NB: No race at Class 3 or below will have prize money of less than £2,450 (Chase), £2,250 (Hurdles), £1,850 (NH Flat) and £1,150 (Hunter Chase).

- **RIDER TYPE**
Races may be limited to amateur, apprentice (Flat), conditional (National Hunt), or lady riders and these contests yield different trends in some instances.

- **THE DISTANCE OF RACES**
Many experts consider that different techniques are required depending on whether one is betting on the outcome of a sprint or a long-distance race. It is not uncommon for a backer to possess a superior record when betting in races of a certain distance.

Ability Ratings

The official system of handicap ratings is based on the concept that all horses can be assessed on a numerical scale which enables them to be compared according to their ability. The very best horses on the Flat have ratings in the 130s. The very best Jumps horses have ratings in the 180s. The scales differ because horses carry more weight in Jump races. The average rating of all horses on the Flat is about 60 and the average for jumping is about 95. For example, Frankel (the wonder horse) is rated 135 at the time of writing, which makes him the most able horse in the world. The exact position a horse occupies on the scale is determined by its performances against other animals; the number of (horse) lengths it is beaten by and the distance by which it beats others. Thus, the unit of the scale would be lengths other than for the fact that horses race over a variety of distances (e.g., 5f to 2m6f on the flat). Whereas a single length advantage would constitute a very narrow victory in the Grand National (4m4f), it would be considered far more decisive in a 5f sprint. Because of this, the unit of the scale is lbs, which relates to the saddle weight that horses bear.

The simple premise is that weight slows horses down. It is thought that, as race distance increases, so does the effect of a given weight.

For example, according to the scale, a single pound of weight equates to around one third of a length in a 5f sprint but just over one length in the case of a two-mile race. I estimated these figures by using a simple equation (below) which affords us an approximate value. However, the techniques that real handicappers use are far more sophisticated.

lbs beaten = $\dfrac{\textbf{Distance beaten in lengths * 15}}{\textbf{Distance of race in furlongs}}$

A horse needs to have run three times or to have won on its first or second start before it can receive a handicap mark. Once a horse has attained a mark, it is eligible to run in handicaps. The horse's rating will determine which class of handicap it can enter. On a weekly basis, the handicapper will review the performance of each horse and adjust the beast's rating depending on how it fared in relation to its competitors. Such calculations take into account the effects of weight. For example, if horse A beats horse B by five lengths over 7.5f (equates to 10lb) but horse B carries 10lb more in saddle weight than horse A, then the performances are considered equal.

Phil Smith, head handicapper with the BHA

The subtleties of handicapping comprise an art rather than a science and the subjective opinion of the handicapper often comes into play. For instance, handicappers may use race times to assist them in the evaluation of unexposed horses on their first few public outings. On other occasions, the handicapper would focus on a reliable or consistent horse and use this runner as a yardstick against which to compare the performances of improving animals. The class of a race and the quality of performance normally associated with this class may also be taken into account when assessing form. Thus, handicapping presents a minefield of dialectic alternatives and constitutes a model of selection in itself. In North America, the term *handicapping* has a more generic meaning and refers to the entire process of assessing form and predicting racehorse performance.

There are different types of handicap ratings: The **official mark** is compiled by the BHA (British Horseracing Authority) and is used as the basis for allotting weight in handicap races. Several other private handicaps exist, some of which are affiliated to newspapers such as "postmark", the rating produced by the *Racing Post*. The remits of the private and official handicaps are quite different. The aim of the BHA handicapper is to engender competitive racing and consequently the ideal potential of a horse is assessed. Private handicappers are not accountable to the interests of the horse's connections and therefore have a lot more latitude in determining their marks. Because of this, private ratings normally reflect what a horse has actually achieved rather than what it is potentially capable of. For this reason, the term *ability ratings* applies well to the official BHA mark but not to private handicaps, which can be better thought of as *performance ratings*.

Limitations of handicap rating

Despite the obvious utility of handicap ratings, they are clearly fraught with limitations. Extraneous variables which can dramatically affect performance such as the *going* and the *draw* are difficult to incorporate. Also, horses are often spared once they are out of the prize money places so the distances that separate runners which finish down the field are exaggerated. This is exacerbated by the lack of prize money in lower grades. Lightly raced horses or those with foreign form present a problem for the handicapper, and the resultant ratings are less reliable. The pace of the race may also influence the distance which separates winners: A slow, tactical affair will often flatter the weaker horses which finish close up.

The utility of ratings

Ratings constitute a very potent and simple variable for use in systematic betting approaches as they represent a shorthand for ability and performance. Indeed, of all the different statistical information that exists about a given horse, ratings are generally the most significant. The principle behind some of my best results has been to identify occasions when the betting public underestimates a horse which is nonetheless highly rated. Whereas handicap ratings cannot always be used to identify the likely winner of a race, they can serve to point out horses that are highly likely to lose. In this way, ratings function as a "wide filter" providing a fast means of narrowing down a field of runners. Whether one is spending time analysing form before a race or entering data into a computer programme, it certainly helps to eliminate half the field in one fell swoop. However, the more expert and knowledgeable a backer becomes, the less likely they are to depend on ratings and the more likely they are to consider the various moderating factors that affect racehorse performance such as the suitability of today's conditions.

Speed Ratings

*"Speed ratings will help you understand the differing abilities
of racehorses in a way nothing else ever will"*
Nick Mordin

An alternative to scales of ability that are based purely on margins
of victory and defeat is speed ratings, which are determined by the
times that horses take to complete their races. The advantage of
speed ratings is that they constitute an absolute measure against an
objective standard. As with private handicap ratings, speed figures
are of particular importance in certain types of races. On turf there
are many tactical, slow races that are not "truly" run; hence, slow
times do not always indicate a lack of ability whereas a fast time
generally marks a good performance.

The concept of assessing performance according to the objective
criterion of race times is appealing. There is no doubt that, when
expertly compiled, speed ratings provide adept backers with
a decisive edge. The conventional handicap scale is somewhat
exposed; it is quite easy for most punters to discern the distances
that have separated horses in previous races, even if it is necessary
to use collateral form. Therefore, handicap ratings are generally
incorporated into the prices on offer and opportunities for profit
are limited. Race times on the other hand are relatively hidden from
view; it is unusual for them to be discussed at length in the racing
press. When speed is referred to prominently then this is normally
because of a fast time (e.g., a course record) that could simply have
been due to firm ground. Furthermore, it is generally not apparent
from watching a race whether a fast time has been recorded or not.

The older all-weather surface *Fibresand* and, to a lesser extent,
the newer *Polytrack* do not permit the same level of acceleration
that turf does and, consequently, races are run in a more evenly-
paced manner so it is vital to travel well. For example, on Southwell's

Fibresand it is very hard for a leading animal to be caught. It follows that speed figures are of greater importance when considering a bet in an all-weather race. In jump racing the race distances are relatively longer with tactics and jockeyship entering into the equation to a greater extent. Hence, speed ratings are of somewhat lesser importance and should be subjected to greater scrutiny.

Compilation of speed ratings

There are many methods of concocting speed ratings but they share common foundations. Rather than relay an abstract formula or specialised approach, I offer a very simple account of the mechanics that underlie speed figures in general. Without question, a time recorded in a 5f race on the sweeping downhill track at Epsom is not comparable with a time clocked on the stern, uphill 5f course at neighbouring Sandown. Due to the different characteristics of each racecourse, it is necessary to correct race times in order to take into account the *standard time* that applies to each distance that is run at every racecourse. There are different ways of compiling a standard time. For example, on the *Racing Post* database the term refers to the time that would be expected of a moderate horse (e.g., rated 100 on the flat) when carrying nine stones in weight and running on good ground.

In practice, maintaining a list of standard times is an incredibly painstaking task which is made considerably less efficient by the fact that racecourses in Europe do not report race distances accurately. For this reason, a whole network of forums has sprung up discussing the impromptu movement of running rails and all manner of other variances which might need to be taken into account. For each race, we arrive at a speed figure that expresses the winner's performance in relation to the standard time (number of seconds faster or slower). The speed figure must be expressed *per furlong* in order that races of varying distance may be compared. For instance, a performance over a mile that is one second under the standard time would equate to a time that is two seconds below standard in a two-mile race, and so on. It is worth noting that the standard time is not always an "average" of sorts, for example the *Racing Post*'s "standard" (as described above) generally represents a very fast run. Hence, most runs are slower than "standard". This is not an issue in itself as the standard is intended to reflect the *standardised* differences between each racecourse and trip rather than a standard level of performance that horses should achieve.

Understandably, race times are slower when the going is soft. Indeed, "slow" and "fast" are considered to be categories of going in some racing nations. The influence of the ground on times is accounted for by calculating a *going allowance*: the times for each race on a given card are compared to standard times in order to assess the extent to which today's clockings are collectively slower or faster than expected. Standard times are not the only reference point that can be used when determining the going allowance. Instead, it is possible to compare today's race times against those recorded in similar races at the course in question (e.g., maiden races for three-year-olds in Class 3). Once calculated, the going allowance is used to correct the speed figure by effectively eliminating the influence of the ground. By way of criticism, the going allowance for each fixture has to be calculated from a very small sample size and is thus affected by the vagaries of individual races, not all of which may be truly run.

For the sake of clarity, the final speed figure is normally converted into the same scale of weight that is used in conventional handicap ratings. This procedure results in a rating for the winner of the race. In order to determine the ratings for each other runner, points are deducted according to the distance (in lbs) which each horse was beaten by the winner. Because the weight scale is generally used, the differences in saddle weight between the runners can then be accounted for in the manner previously described.

Lengths and seconds

A question that is intrinsic to the establishment of speed ratings is "how long does it take to run a length?" Which in itself begs the question, "how long is a length?" Annoyingly, there is no standard metric for a length. Estimates vary from between eight and 11 feet, depending on the calculations of the rater. However, since horses are moving at different speeds and generally slowing down as they finish, the distance between them is changing. To avoid this uncertainty, the reported distance in lengths is often conceived of as a unit of *time* (for example, one length = 0.2 seconds). In fact, **0.2** is an approximation that held prominence for many years. In recent times, more sophisticated methods have sprung up and a range of **0.167 to 0.20** seconds is reportedly used depending on various factors such as the race length.

Because, like race distances, the official lengths reported by racecourses are often inaccurate, some raters attempt to record actual times for each finisher. In fairness, all methods that rely on speed ratings suffer from the same blight of poor information; often the remedy is perspicacity and an incredible amount of hard work! There has been some progress since my last book. In June 2008, the BHA introduced a more sophisticated method of reporting lengths. The winning distances are calculated by a photo-finish computer using a formula based on time as each horse crosses the line. The exact time-distance formulae (lengths per second scale) appear in Table 3.

TABLE 3: LENGTHS PER SECOND SCALE

FLAT-TURF	L.P.S
GOOD OR QUICKER	6
GOOD, GOOD TO SOFT IN PLACES / GOOD TO SOFT, GOOD IN PLACES / GOOD TO SOFT / GOOD TO SOFT, SOFT IN PLACES	5.5
SOFT, GOOD TO SOFT IN PLACES / SOFT OR SLOWER	5

FLAT-AWT	
KEMPTON, LINGFIELD, WOLVERHAMPTON	6
GREAT LEIGHS	5.5
SOUTHWELL	5
JUMPS	
GOOD OR QUICKER	4
GOOD, GOOD TO SOFT IN PLACES / GOOD TO SOFT, GOOD IN PLACES / GOOD TO SOFT / GOOD TO SOFT, SOFT IN PLACES	4.5
SOFT, GOOD TO SOFT IN PLACES / SOFT OR SLOWER	4
NH FLAT (AWT)	
KEMPTON, LINGFIELD	5
SOUTHWELL	4

* Going changes during the day may alter the scale to be applied. Ensure the clerk of scales and course alert you to any changes.
* When the going description distinguishes between different parts of the course, apply the scale relating to the going in the straight.

Sectional times

Another bone of contention between the punting cognoscenti and the racecourses is the failure to provide the sectional times which our transatlantic cousins regard as *de rigeur*. Such information is, of course, essential to the judgement of pace, which is in itself a whole avenue of selection. We have witnessed several false dawns when it comes to the advent of sectional timing. In fact, every book I have written contains mention of a trial or some promised development which ultimately wilted and died. This time around I can report that *At The Races* and Southwell racecourse produced sectional times in October 2010 as a trial. The outcry over the lack of sectional times for Frankel's electrifying win in the 2000 Guineas of 2011 has prompted meeting sponsors QIPCO to finance the installation of a sectional timing system at Ascot in time for the British Champions Day on 15 October. So perhaps there is some cause for encouragement. In fairness, the installation of equipment across the country would not come at an insignificant cost. Yet there seems to be a missed opportunity in my eyes. Clearly, there is a market for these times, and I would argue it is possible to collate them without going the whole hog and putting chips in saddlecloths. Cue an enterprising individual.

The *Split Second* speed ratings

Not all speed ratings incorporate saddle weight in the conventional way. For example, the *Split Second* speed ratings compiled by the *Racing Post*'s Dave Bellingham are somewhat more advanced and thus merit explanation. Rather than weight, the ratings are expressed in terms of lengths-per-mile. In order to calculate the standard times, Dave uses median winning times over a particular trip going back several years. The criterion used is a minimum of 20 races over the trip in the past five seasons or less. Following a meeting, a "raw", unadjusted speed rating is calculated for each winner on the card (i.e., how many lengths-per-mile the winning time differed from the standard time for the trip). A difference of ⅕ second equates to one length. The "raw" speed ratings are then compared to a 'par' figure for the class of race (e.g., Class 1) which represents a time that should be achievable for the average winner in that class of race. In this way the standard times take into account the class of horses.

To calculate the going allowance, the differences between the "raw" speed ratings and the par figures for each race are examined. The fastest and slowest races compared to "par" are discarded and the remainder are then averaged. This figure indicates the extent to which the elements and the going have affected the final times of each race. The going allowance is then used to adjust the raw speed figures and produce the final rating, which represents how fast the winners would have run on a perfectly good surface with no external influences such as the weather. The ratings for beaten horses are calculated by adjusting for the number of lengths they finished behind the winner. Notably, the *Split Second* ratings do not take into account the effect of weight, either historically or on the current racecard. This component is left completely at the user's discretion.

My speed method

There are many different ways to utilise race times without constructing speed ratings. To illustrate this point I came up with a simple technique that I explained in *Against The Odds*. Essentially, I sought to circumvent the twin problems of standard times and going allowances by waiting until I found a race with two runners which had recorded recent times that could be directly compared (i.e., same course, distance, and going). This is not as rare an occurrence as intuition dictates it should be. Quite often two horses will visit the same course and run in similar contests as part of their preparation for a big race. It is debatable whether one can say with confidence that two horses have indeed raced over exactly the same ground. However, this limitation is the only real hair in the soup; as long as the two races in question were run at the same course then minor discrepancies between the two distances and going reports can be tolerated. Of course, it is not enough to simply find an occasion when two runners in a race have recorded recent times under similar conditions: the real rub is to pinpoint an unexposed or unfancied horse that has produced a time similar to or better than that recorded by one of the market leaders in a race. This denotes value. I have learnt that this angle is very useful at the Cheltenham Festival, precisely because the principals often run trials at Prestbury Park, not to mention their festival appearances the year before!

The Effects of Weight

Is it valid to express the differences between horses in terms of lbs?

The manner in which weight is factored into handicap ratings would seem to suggest that the effect of weight on performance is a universal constant. Consider the case of two horses of precisely equal ability that run an endless succession of 5f races without fatigue. If the first horse were to carry an extra pound of weight, would it really lose by the exact $\frac{1}{3}$ of a length that the handicapper predicts it should. Furthermore, if one kept adding weight to the saddlecloth of the first horse, would the animal proceed to lose each race by a margin that was in exact proportion to weight added? Would this principle operate similarly for all horses of different physiques in a universal way?

The horse's quadrupedal gait, strength, and efficiency of movement make it marvellously suited to bearing loads; a characteristic that has defined the human-equine relationship for thousands of years. What difference is a 3lb penalty really going to make to animal of some 1,200lbs, especially when the animal in question is a beast of burden and the weight is well positioned above the horse's centre of gravity? Nick Mordin has demonstrated that weight only encumbers horses significantly when they are travelling at *maximum speed*; our equine friends slow considerably to undertake turns and thus weight is a greater issue when horses are racing in a straight line.

The ratings that appear in newspapers and formbook publications are typically adjusted for the weight that horses are set to carry in forthcoming races. Hence, if a horse that is rated 10lbs clear of the field is carrying a penalty of 3lbs in weight relative to the other runners, then the animal's advantage is thought to be only 7lbs. Whereas handicap races are characterised by the weight differential across the runners, non-handicap races are also riddled with various types of weight penalty and allowance. In conditions races, penalties are allotted on the basis of past performances, such as wins in races over a certain value. Younger horses and fillies generally benefit from a weight allowance that is thought to redress the natural advantage possessed by their elder and male peers respectively. The current weight-for-age scales appear at the rear of this book for reference purposes.

In the past, I have completely ignored the different weights carried by runners, as this has given me better results than when I have tried to factor them in. I used a statistical technique to retrospectively adjust handicap ratings and found that the optimal level of correction lies between 0.25lbs and 0.50lbs. In other words, weight impedes horses between two and four time less than the current system assumes. The real problem is not the correction that is made to the ratings of runners in a forthcoming race; that can easily be eliminated or reversed. The difficulty lies in the fact that weight corrections have been used all the way through the process of compiling the ratings. Although I do not disagree in principle with a rating system that evaluates the performances of horses based on the distances they win and lose by, I do not think that such a system should be scaled by weight. The minimal effects of weight should be accounted for and analysed separately.

Handicap Races

A horse climbing the handicap scale will either carry a heavier weight against similar rivals in its next race or face tougher competition. It is worth nothing that if a horse wins a handicap it will have to carry a winner's penalty if running again before the revised handicap is published (which is on a Tuesday morning). When a horse *consistently* fails to run up to its mark, its rating is gradually reduced. As such, competitive racing is the ultimate objective of the handicapper and the canon of his merit. The classification structure of handicaps was revised in 2008 to streamline its bands and clarify the distinction between them in terms of prize money (see Tables 1 and 2). In order to foster keener competition, the weight differential of handicaps was restricted to a narrower band of between 14lbs (Flat) and 15 lbs (Jumps). There are some exceptions to this rule, including the valuable "heritage" handicaps such as the Lincoln and Cesarewitch, which have retained their broad weight differentials.

What mark is it on?

Clearly, the most fundamental selection criterion in handicap races is the mark a horse is on vis-à-vis its past performances. Has the animal won or come close to winning a race comparable with today's off a similar mark? The plentiful nature of handicap form provides us with a huge amount of data to work with. In contrast to the process of selection for non-handicaps, recent form is of lesser importance. Handicappers seem to peak and trough and the clues pointing towards a horse's chances may be 16 months ago when it last raced off a mark this low on the same track and won. Most handicappers have a ceiling; they can win up to a certain mark and once this point has been reached they need to descend back down the handicap in order to become competitive. And descend they do, very slowly.

Expresso Star wins the 2009 Lincoln Handicap

Betting in handicaps

Handicap races are inherently trickier than stakes races. The fields are larger, the races are more competitive, and then there's the quasi-religion of the handicap system itself. Nevertheless, most successful backers actually favour handicaps. There is a lot of form available as most handicappers run regularly in similar company and are therefore quite exposed. This amount of information can provide opportunities for experienced bettors to gain a foothold and establish an edge over less methodical gamblers. The amount of effort that bookmakers expend on promoting handicaps (sponsorship, promotion, advance prices) suggests that these races generate a high level of profit for them. So it follows that the betting public does not fare well in handicaps even though their competitive nature ensures that they are very popular betting fodder. This greater interest translates into more liquidity, which is beneficial to the serious backer.

The reason for the equivocality of handicap form lies in the essential nature of the handicap system, which functions to punish ability. A handicap mark is there to be protected and a trainer might run the horse outside the code or over different obstacles in order to preserve it. Every year, at least one of the principal challengers for the Grand National engages in a hurdles race as a warm-up for Aintree. *Ballabriggs* took in a hurdles race in 2011 as did other recent winners *Silver Birch*, *Numbersixvalverde*, *Hedgehunter*, and *Monty's Pass*. There is a huge incentive for those connected with horses (i.e., owners and trainers) to run an animal in unsuitable conditions so as to achieve a low handicap mark which can then be exploited. The simplest method to vouchsafe a weak run is to enter a horse in a race that confounds the beast's preferences.

Ballabriggs on his way to winning the 2011 Grand National

The competitive nature of handicaps is not really determined by the weight differential but by the fact that horses of similar ability are being brought together. Even within the handicap sphere there are variants thought to be particularly opaque from the backer's point of view. For instance, it is often remarked that sprint handicappers take it in turns to win their races. The equivalent contest under National Hunt rules would be the two-mile handicap hurdle. David Ashforth once wrote that with three hours of hard work one might hope to narrow down the field in such a race to 20 possibles. Handicaps can prove to be the graveyard of the inexperienced backer. So always regard handicaps and stakes races as very distinct entities. I have found that betting approaches transfer very poorly from one arena to the other.

Racing journalist David Ashforth

Headgear

Headgear is one of those irritating little variables in racing that could mean everything or nothing. You'd love to dismiss it completely but it still plays on your mind. Before I did any research into headgear my stock view was that it is a negative; a kind of quackery that trainers dabble in because they don't know any better. If I was wavering on a selection, then noticed the horse was wearing blinkers, I would happily put a line through it. Of course, it's never that simple. Horses are every bit as individual as people.

I think part of my antipathy to backing horses in headgear comes from the significance that armchair punters place on these devices. There's a serious point in there: maybe the profits that are there to be made by backing or opposing horses in headgear come not so much from the effect of these devices on performance but from the influence they have on the behaviour of betting folk. Trainers and owners understand these reactions, and often when betting coups have been recounted, it transpires that headgear has been used to throw punters off the scent. Blinkers or a visor might serve to mask some unexpected improvement, or even to convey the impression that the trainer has lost patience with the horse.

My view here is that headgear affects pace judgement in a serious way especially in longer contests such as chases over two circuits. This is particularly true at Cheltenham where I have witnessed many horses with blinkers doing too much on the first circuit and then getting swallowed up before the turn for home. Views on headgear must go hand in hand with views on race tactics and jockeyship. In jump racing, there are plenty of contests in which strong front-runners triumph when the tyres seem to bounce off everything else. *Our Vic*'s Ryanair chase triumph in 2008 is a case in point. The blinkers went along with a change of tactics. It seemed as if he might have hit the wall turning in but he picked up well. The blinkers helped him to be where he needed to be in the race and kept him to his task.

Although there are general trends, headgear is definitely a subject that cries out for a horse-by-horse perspective. Holding the view that blinkers are bad per se can end up costing you money. A case in point was the Grand National of 2008 which was won by a blinkered animal, *Comply or Die*. The National is the archetypal "trends" race and one of the strongest of these relates to headgear: since *L'Escargot* in 1975, only one horse with blinkers had triumphed before 2008. In all other respects *Comply or Die* was a very strong candidate on my shortlist of four. Five years before I would have overlooked him without a shadow of a doubt. This time I backed him, albeit to a smaller stake, because the headgear seemed to work well for the horse. He had been rejuvenated by blinkers on testing ground at Haydock and went on to win a long-distance chase in the *Eider*, beating 17 rivals. So the clues were there. I contend that headgear is misused more often than not, but it has its place.

Comply or Die (left) and D'Argent, both wearing blinkers

Finishing Positions and Margins of Victory

Although often given prominence, as a statistic the *finishing position* has numerous disadvantages. It is better to finish second in a field of 30 runners than in a field of three runners, yet both performances appear the same in black type. It is possible for a horse to be beaten into second place by 30 lengths while a different animal might finish seventh yet be only a couple of lengths distant from the winner. From a psychological point of view, that "2" or "3" printed next to the horse's name in the newspaper is very beguiling. Because the finishing position is such a visible characteristic of each runner, there is a possibility that we can make it work in our favour by exploiting the tendency of punters to take it at face value.

Although winning distances are of course catered for within the framework of ability ratings, they do constitute a variable in their own right, not least because the margin of victory is highly publicised and may influence betting patterns in subsequent races. One generally encounters two opposing schools of thought on the subject of winning distances: A large margin of victory may indicate sheer ability or just a lack of competition. Those who subscribe to the latter view prefer to follow horses that are involved in battling finishes, even if they are just touched off.

Trainers

The potential for physical development in the Thoroughbred is exceptional and it is the trainer who crafts and shapes the raw substance of each horse. Indeed, identifying the circumstances under which each trainer's string performs well leads to a significant betting edge not least because such trends often pinpoint winners that have not shown particularly good public form. If the entire racehorse population were divided randomly between the many training establishments then we would know who the better trainers were. Instead, the success of a yard depends, to a large degree, on the quality of horses therein. Nevertheless, the skills and practices of each trainer are idiosyncratic and shape the ability and development of the horses in their care. Trainers prepare their horses for races in markedly different ways. Furthermore, each handler enjoys varying degrees of success with specific types of runners and races. This is why it is not true to think that the trainer's influence will be fully accounted for by the previous form that a horse has shown.

The skill of the trainer also manifests itself in the way horses are campaigned. These stratagems are characteristic of each trainer, and they lead to patterns of results which can be exploited for profit. A further source of encouragement is the huge public bias towards popular trainers. This bias disturbs the market and can result in favourable prices if one is prepared to refrain from backing horses that are trained by the big potatoes in the racing field.

Trainers' characteristics

A popular approach is to break down the performance of a trainer's runners by racetrack, animal type (maidens, juveniles, etc.), or even the type of race (novice chases for example). Often these variables are stacked together so that we consider, for instance, how David Pipe does with his novice hurdlers at Newton Abbot. A worry associated with this approach is that we are straying into the territory of small sample sizes and back-fitting. Hence, extra caution is needed.

Nevertheless, the trends we uncover can be extremely potent as they reflect the underlying modus operandi of the trainer, and trainers are creatures of habit in the extreme. By understanding the way the trainer's place their charges we gain an insight into their private opinion of each runner's merits. While this might not be the whole story, it is nonetheless a potent clue as to the animal's potential. One such "clue" which can prove decisive is the performance of a handler in a *specific race* over several seasons. There are obvious examples pertaining to Group 1 and Grade 1 races in the public eye, but I am referring to lesser-known races at provincial tracks. These patterns can sometimes prove the most revealing because here is proof that the trainer in question knows exactly what it takes to win these unique events. Their entries will therefore be carefully planned and worthy of attention.

Jockeys

Good jockeys cannot win without good horses although poor riding can certainly squander a winning chance; the horsemanship of riders like AP McCoy being the exception that neatly proves the rule. Jockeys do not affect the performances of horses to the same extent that trainers do. However, this does not stop the betting public from placing their utmost faith in the top riders; a bias that can create opportunities for the shrewd backer.

Champion jockey AP McCoy

How do you discern the ability of a jockey? With great difficulty. A jockey's performance in terms of strike rate is largely dependent on the stature of the trainer for whom he typically rides. AP McCoy's awesome reputation was built on the quality and quantity of runners provided by the champion trainer of the time, Martin Pipe. Success bred success. The standing that AP earned from riding Pipe's horses enabled him to acquire very promising rides from other trainers to supplement his wining total. As was the case with his successor Timmy Murphy, McCoy clearly earned the right to ride for Pipe. But for the vast majority of other jockeys, riding the more able horses may prove a difficult vault to gain access into. Various methods of assessing the true relative merits of jockeys have been attempted, most of which entail drawing a comparison between two riders using a mount they have both ridden as a yardstick. These approaches generally prove disappointing, not least because there is a low signal to noise ratio. There are so many other factors besides horsemanship to cloud the analysis such as the way riders are "jocked" off.

Apprentice and conditional riders

Until they gain a full professional licence, apprentice (Flat) and conditional (Jumps) jockeys claim an allowance in terms of a weight advantage over their fully fledged counterparts. Apprentices claim 7lbs until they have won 20 races, thereafter 5lbs until they have won 50 races, and finally 3lbs until they have won 95 races, at which point they are eligible to apply for a full professional licence. Conditional jockeys racing under National Hunt rules lose their 7lb, 5lb, and 3lb claims after they have won 20, 40, and 75 races respectively. It will not surprise you to learn that I think the weight advantage fairly irrelevant. Nevertheless, an apprentice's weight claim may prompt a trainer to put up an inexperienced jockey on a heavily weighted runner in a handicap; a tactic that generally proves unwise.

The Going

Phil Bull, the father of *Timeform*, felt that the going preferences of a horse should be the most important consideration when making a selection. The complex gait of our equine friends means they have a huge potential for developing distinct preferences for racing surfaces. When they show Jekyll and Hyde form the most likely explanation is the going. It goes without saying that such fluctuations are massively significant to the value-seeker because they can serve to completely nullify a horse's best form. Take for example the popular middle-distance chaser *Albertas Run*. The results in Table 4 need no comment.

TABLE 4: RECENT PERFORMANCES OF ALBERTAS RUN BY GOING

Date	Course	Grade	Ground	Position	SP
08-Apr-11	Aintree	Grade 1	Good	2/10 (9L Master Minded)	11/4F
17-Mar-11	Cheltenham	Grade 1	Good	1/11 (1L Kalahari King)	6/1
15-Jan-11	Kempton	Grade 1	Good to Soft	PU/9 (Long Run)	33/1
20-Nov-10	Ascot	Grade 2	Good to Soft	F/6 (Master Minded)	9/4
23-Oct-10	Aintree	Grade 2	Good to Soft	4/6 (45L Monet's Garden)	11/2
09-Apr-10	Aintree	Grade 1	Good	1/11 (3¼L Forpadydeplasterer)	8/1
18-Mar-10	Cheltenham	Grade 1	Good	1/13 (4½L Poquelin)	14/1
20-Feb-10	Ascot	Grade 1	Good to Soft	2/6 (1½L Monet's Garden)	13/2
26-Dec-09	Kempton	Grade 1	Good to Soft	6/13 (69L Kauto Star)	25/1
10-Dec-09	Huntingdon	Grade 2	Good to Soft	3/7 (11L Deep Purple)	7/2
21-Nov-09	Ascot	Grade 2	Good	1/8 (3L Planet Of Sound)	7/1

The effects of the elements and watering on turf are self explanatory, but artificial surfaces require more in the way of an explanation. In general terms, rain and moisture tend to compact and harden the artificial surfaces. Synthetic topsoils (i.e., *Fibresand* and *Polytrack*) respond to moisture and wear in different ways. The looser *Fibresand* (currently laid at Southwell) wears more easily than *Polytrack* (Lingfield, Kempton, and Wolverhampton), a wax-coated synthetic riding surface that regains its original shape extremely well after hoof penetration and is less susceptible to the effects of extreme weather.

Track management of the surface also plays a role. Taking Southwell as an example, the surface was re-laid in 2004 to provide a better

Albertas Run with Tony McCoy on his way to winning the 2011 Ryanair Chase at Cheltenham

consistency across all parts of the track and more work took place in September 2010, when the surface was substantially reconfigured. Such work makes a noticeable difference to the going (and would certainly have an impact on the compilation of speed figures). While we're on the subject of Southwell, when the temperature dips below zero the course is ploughed to ensure it does not freeze. This practice has the effect of loosening the surface and making it much slower.

It is often remarked that extremes of going affect the likelihood that a race will be run according to established form. For example, when the ground is heavy, emphasis is placed on the ability of runners to cope with the conditions underfoot and this effect appears to randomise results. Conversely, firm ground is thought to aid favourites and form horses in flat races. The picture is rather different where jumping is concerned, with a consensus that ground on the soft side of good produces the most reliable results as this typifies the seasonal weather.

All-weather racing at Southwell

Assessing the going preferences of a runner is a deceptively demanding task. In practice, much interpretation is required. For example, if you review a chaser's form and note that it won a hurdles race three years ago on the same heavy going that it will encounter again today, it is easy to jump to the conclusion (excuse the pun) that the prevailing conditions are suitable. However, the hurdles race may have been a poor contest (e.g., amateur race, seller, mares race) against only two other runners. Another easy error to commit is being too quick to assign going preferences to a juvenile horse. A lot of trainers like to "run a horse in" so as to build up a handicap mark. For this reason, one bad run on soft ground in a three-year-old maiden race does not necessarily mean that the beast is averse to slower surfaces. Class appears to interact with going in that classier types can act on almost any ground and it's often only poorer specimens that need "their conditions" in order to succeed.

Going reports

The real issue facing backers when considering the state of the ground is the sheer equivocality of going reports. They can be so wildly and patently inaccurate as to be of no use whatsoever. This creates an issue for system testers as it becomes almost impossible to locate historical trends due to noise in the data. Going reports by their nature are complex beasts, they take into account factors such as the weather conditions at the time of the assessment, the forecasted weather, and any irrigation that has been, or is yet to be applied. Also, the clerks are following the BHA directive to aim for what is considered the safest ground (Good-to-Firm on the flat, and Good over the sticks). Coupled with this, there is a strong imperative for racecourses to attract runners and avoid desertions by owners and trainers. The upshot of this is that the going report sometimes conveys what the course would like the going to be. As part of my role as a horseracing trader I was in regular contact before racing with the clerks of each course and their offices. I found that the going was quite often described to me as being markedly different to the official forecast. I found after a time that I was able to presage the likely going by looking at the weather satellite myself and considering what I had been told over the phone by the clerk's team.

The Going Stick

The Going Stick is intended to compliment the official going report as a scientific measure of the resistance provided by the turf and its degree of "shear", a term that refers to the amount of force required to pull the stick down to a 45 degree angle from an upright position. Three measurements are taken from up to 80 points on the course (60 on the flat) and an aggregate reading calculated. The device produces a numerical reading that varies between 1.0 (heavy) and 15.0 (hard); a figure that can easily be easily translated into the conventional going categories that we know and love.

The Going Stick in action

Guide to Going Stick Categories

1.0 - 2.9 = Heavy   3.0 - 4.9 = Soft

5.0 - 6.9 = Good to Soft   7.0 - 8.9 = Good

9.0 - 10.9 = Good to Firm   11.0 - 12.9 = Firm

13.0 - 15.0 = Hard

To compliment the guide, here are the mean Going Stick readings associated with each type of going for both flat and jumps racing (see Table 5):

TABLE 5: MEAN GOING STICK RATINGS by OFFICIAL GOING REPORTS

OFFICIAL GOING DESCRIPTION GIVEN BY CLERK OF COURSE	JUMPS		FLAT	
	Number of reports logged	Mean going stick Reading	Number of reports logged	Mean going stick reading
HEAVY	210	5.2	68	5.5
SOFT	499	6	258	6.4
GOOD TO SOFT	672	6.9	581	7.1
GOOD	1089	8	1165	8
GOOD TO FIRM	543	9	1538	8.9
FIRM	10	10.5	150	10.1
HARD	0	N/A	0	N/A

NB: Where an official going description given by a Clerk of the Course falls between two possible ground descriptions (for example: 'Good, good to firm in places'), the first and therefore predominant ground description (in this case "Good") is used for statistical purposes.

It is important to recognise that soil type and drainage differ markedly between courses, so the actual *Going Stick* reading that corresponds to genuine good ground is not consistent. Added to this is the fact that the going may differ dramatically across different parts of the course and on opposite sides of the track.

Any change in the state of the ground becomes apparent from watching the horses' actions, especially when they approach the final furlong and fatigue begins to set in. It is worth closely observing the depth of the imprint that the hooves make in the turf. Another pointer is when the first race or two on the card go to unexpected winners with better form on soft ground. One of the reasons I enjoy betting at Cheltenham is that the racecourse provides a radio service that enables me to hear interviews with the trainers in the parade ring via a small earpiece. Valuable information regarding the true going can be gleaned from the comments of trainers and jockeys.

Arguably, the most potent method of assessing the ground is to examine race times. Notably, going that has been officially described as "good" has produced times which vary quite alarmingly. It is especially illuminating to investigate finishing times after the first day of a big festival meeting and conclude that the going is slower or faster than advertised. Going is a mysterious concept, as the poor performance of a horse that has much winning form under the prevailing conditions can still be excused by its trainer because it "didn't like the ground".

The Racecourse

The huge variation in the characteristics of the 60 British racecourses means that one must assess the extent to which the form from one course will transfer to another. Indeed, this aspect of betting methodology has drifted into the vernacular ("horses for courses"). A classic example is provided every year when racing "personalities" debate the likelihood that the winner of the 2000 Guineas on Newmarket's wide, flat, Rowley Mile course will handle Epsom's tight, roller-coaster Derby course. Horses are highly sensitive to their environment and success on a certain type of course is a product of the animal's preferences as well as the configuration of its physique. Fortunately, the neat categories that are used to describe the features of racecourses render this a subject highly suitable for statistical analysis. The distinguishing characteristics of each course are various:

- **Direction of turns:** Left-handed, right-handed, or a combination of both.
- **Undulation:** Ranging from the pancake flatness of Kempton Park to the alpine topography of Epsom or Goodwood.
- **Inclination of finish:** An uphill finish such as that of Cheltenham can prove to be a particular test of stamina.

- **Tightness of turns:** Ranging from the centrifugal circuit at Chester to the roman straightness of Newmarket's Rowley mile.
- **Length of finishing straight:** A less significant factor that can nevertheless affect the shape and outcome of races.
- **Width of track:** Whereas Newbury's track is as wide as a country mile, the finishing straights at Goodwood and Pontefract are particularly narrow.
- **Size, construction, spacing, and types of fences:** The different designations of fence include water jumps, plain fences, and open ditches.

The Time of Year
The shape of the racing year

The flat season begins with a flourish in late March, on the day of the Lincoln handicap held at Doncaster. From this point, the drama unfolds in several distinct phases until the curtain falls in the autumn. The November handicap, held on the first Saturday of the month, marks the traditional point when the season returns to its beginnings at Doncaster and the cycle is complete. Due to the programme of summer jump racing, the National Hunt calendar spans the entire year. However, the diluted schedule of summer racing on faster ground is very much an interlude; there are no truly major races and the majority of horses are rested and prepared for a winter campaign.

In the months between May and September, jumps racing sleeps with one eye open. The first significant meeting of the winter season is the Paddy Power Open at Cheltenham, which is normally held on the second weekend in November. From this point onwards there is a measured build up towards the crescendo of the championship races that fill a four-day festival in mid-March back at Cheltenham. Aintree's Grand National meeting in early April serves as a climax to the season and offers many races that are commensurate in value to their Cheltenham equivalents. The Bet365 (formerly Whitbread) Gold Cup, contested at Sandown on the last weekend in April, is the final valuable race and marks the ultimate day of the season. Symbolically, the card at Sandown on that day is "mixed" and includes both flat and jumps races. After this equinox, the baton of our attention is passed on to the flat while jumps racing trots off to the summer pastures of Stratford, Uttoxeter and Market Rasen.

The flat season on the turf is characterised by a string of celebrated meetings at courses such as Doncaster, Newmarket (Rowley Mile and July courses), Chester, York, Ascot, Goodwood, Epsom, Newbury and Sandown. The shape of the season is rather skewed, as it reaches its zenith in June with the Derby and Oaks at Epsom followed very quickly by the Royal Ascot fixture. The final *classic* meeting is held at Doncaster in mid September to accommodate the St Leger. From this point onwards, the season freewheels towards its indeterminate conclusion in early November. Accordingly, the contours of the jumps and flat seasons are most dissimilar: the measured, incremental ascent of the National Hunt calendar resolves into a finale equivalent to the cup final or championship game of a football season. On the contrary, the flat season on the turf takes off like a rocket and burns up on re-entry. Under both codes, the valuable televised races act like coat pegs from which the rest of the season is hung.

While all this is happening, the all-weather season continues like a steady beat in the background. The fixture list limps through the summer from April to October while it is eclipsed by its turf equivalent, albeit less so now that Kempton is staging Polytrack racing. The official winter flat season begins the day after the summer flat season ends and runs until the day before the new summer flat season commences. During this time, around two thirds of all-weather races are held.

Seasonal trends and betting

I have often read that backers should avoid betting at the beginning and end of each season, as profit is less likely. I have also noticed a seasonal trend in my own betting performance whereby I flourish in

May and June but appear to "hit the wall" in July. There are several reasons for this seasonal variation: at the beginning of the season, fields are large and there is no recent form available. The form that is generated by these early races takes a few weeks to settle down as horses rapidly regain full racing fitness or improve on their debut performances while others re-emerge belatedly carrying good condition.

As the summer months draw on, horses that have been heavily campaigned become jaded and those that have been well rested can re-emerge to overturn established form. At the season's end, weather conditions deteriorate once more and opportunities to race become ever sparser. Field sizes increase again as trainers enter their charges for races while they still can. A further type of seasonal trend is caused by the impact of the bigger meetings. As the more able horses are put away for them, and yards gear up for the challenge, results can become chaotic. Festival meetings such as Royal Ascot and Cheltenham also seem to cause a "wake" in their immediate aftermath whereby beasts which have bypassed the big meeting hold the aces and can win at big prices.

Fitness
The physiology of fitness

The term *fitness* covers various types of physical conditioning, which the Thoroughbred develops through the combination of racing, training, nutrition and rest. The development of cardio-vascular and respiratory fitness lay the foundations for more demanding work that promotes improvements in the equine musculo-skeletal system such as increased muscle size, contractile power, co-ordination, and flexibility. The essential principle that underlies such conditioning is one of adaptation. A stress is imposed on the horse and an adaptation occurs so that the physical structure concerned can more readily cope with that stressor in the future. For instance, a five-furlong sprinter will tear thousands of individual muscle fibres during each race and these will be repaired during the horse's recovery. Consequently, the muscles in question will prove marginally more powerful when they are next called upon to contract in a race. When the source of stress is removed, the adaptations become redundant and are reversed so that the body can be more efficient; unnecessary muscle tissue merely wastes energy.

If the intensity, frequency, or duration of the races and training sessions is too high then the horse will be over-trained, its performance will suffer, and its whole immune system will be compromised. Like human marathon runners who undergo intensive training regimens, racehorses are especially vulnerable to viral infection. Thoroughbreds are genetically predestined towards athleticism. However, the price of this superior ability is fragility. Think of cars: I can drive my family saloon over a bump in the road with impunity but if I tried to do the same with a Formula 1 racing car, I would mutilate its computer-assisted suspension system.

Maturation

It is important to realise that, even at the end of its three-year-old season, a horse is not fully mature. The rapid process of equine maturation leads to sharp increases in stamina; seven furlongs represents an endurance event for two-year-olds. Juveniles that demonstrate the stamina to endure that distance will subsequently develop into middle-distance types.

Individual fitness profiles

Unquestionably, each animal possesses a unique tolerance to training and racing: some will thrive on regular work whereas others are of a more delicate persuasion. The latter type requires briefer, less-intense training sessions that are interspersed with long periods of recuperation. Like human athletes, horses are trained in cycles as fitness is built up to a peak that can only be maintained for a relatively short period of time. Living organisms must be periodically relieved of stress in order to continue developing. If one could plot on a graph the performance ratings achieved by a horse in each of its races, the result would not resemble a straight line but a wave containing multiple peaks and depressions. Figure 17 depicts the career trajectory, or *performance curve*, of popular staying hurdler Big Buck's.

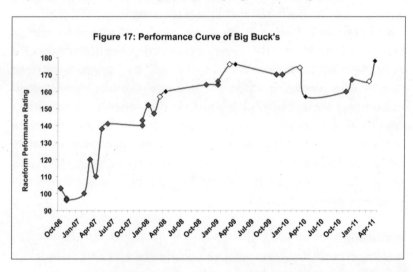

Big Buck's (left) with Ruby Walsh in action at Aintree

On many occasions, poor runs can be explained by unsuitable conditions. However, even if the racing conditions were unchanging, the performance level of a horse would probably not be constant over time. This concept is vital to understand because most bettors look at a series of performances and assume that an improving trend will continue or that a horse will produce a run that is equivalent to its previous effort. Each horse has its own performance curve as unique as a signature and the skill is to anticipate the shape of it based on what you know about the fitness of the horse. This is much like predicting when a share on the stock market has bottomed out or reached its ceiling. Such judgements are made much more possible when you have had the opportunity to see the horse in the flesh at multiple points to assess its physique and the manner of its performances.

Exposure

Exposure is a variable that accounts for the number of races a horse has had in a given period. Quite simply, an overexposed horse has had too many races. A good example of exposure can be found in the elite staying-chasers division in National Hunt racing. There has been a fairly recent trend among trainers like Henrietta Knight and Paul Nicholls to give these beasts very light campaigns, so much so that we might say they are "underexposed". Of course, some horses benefit from exposure and some do not. An example from the current (2011) flat season is provided by Jim Bolger's filly Banimpire (see over). In just five months, the three-year-old has notched up ten Class 1 races across both sides of the Irish Sea including two Group 2 wins, three Group 3 victories, and a triumph in listed company.

Utility of fitness as a selection criterion

The variable of fitness has never led me directly to many winners. But, I have been able to avoid a host of losers and this is of equal importance to my overall profitability. Where possible, I consider

Banimpire with Kevin Manning at the Curragh

fitness on a horse-by-horse basis rather than by trying to apply general rules. A key consideration when appraising the fitness of a horse is the trainer. I find it worthwhile to acquaint myself with the handler's record in developing and maintaining racing fitness in their charges. *The number of days that have elapsed since the previous appearance* appears prominently in racecards, formbooks, and the racing press. Accordingly, there are several prejudices concerning the probability of success for runners returning after a very short (<8 days) or very long (>300 days) lay off, which in itself presents opportunities for profit.

The Draw
The significance of the draw
The drawn allocation of starting stalls is a vital factor to consider when contemplating a bet on the outcome of a flat race. Although the draw doesn't impact upon every race, in many contests the inherent bias can make the difference between winning and losing. Even in races where no draw bias is expected, the previous form of the runners may well have been shaped by the influence of the draw on other courses. The subject is a constant source of interest among betting folk because, by its very nature, the bias is always shifting

and creating opportunities to gain an edge in the fight for profits.

Due to its variable nature, the most relevant evidence of a bias is the most recent – ideally on the same day. Festival meetings often provide the opportunity to seize onto these ephemeral patterns. Research into the effect of racing from different starting stalls first rose to prominence in the United States where it became a veritable science long before the topic was popularised in Britain and Ireland. The contemporary preoccupation with the draw in this country was ignited by the work of several eminent backers, in particular Graham Wheldon, who became synonymous with the subject after the publication of a series of books. The premise of backing favourably drawn horses is disarmingly simple but therein lies the problem. Raw data reveal trends that are often ambiguous and require very careful interpretation. In most cases, other related factors such as the going and the field size need to be taken into account.

The effects of the draw in action at York

Racing publications are infested with superficial treatments of the draw's effects which have become meaningless and token: "Back high-drawn horses at Beverley but not at Chester". Ironically, the awareness gained by the betting public has rendered many formerly profitable draws of no use. Simplistic rules fail to do justice to the subtlety and complexity of the draw's effects. Indeed, copious books have been written on the subject of the draw alone. The position of a horse in the starting stalls provides us with an important clue as to how the runner concerned will be incorporated into the race. It comes back to chaos theory, a race is a sequence of connected events and the initial place that a horse assumes in the field will predetermine its opportunities to succeed in the latter stages of the contest. Energy expended in order to gain a position at the start of the race can exert a disproportionate effect on fatigue levels in the closing stages. Furthermore, energy wasted due to encumbrance in running can predispose a horse to rapid fatigue when an effort is required towards the business end of a race.

The factors that determine the effects of the draw bias:

1) **Curvature of the track:** Acquiring the coveted position on the inside rail around turns often depends on the draw. The horses running on the outside flank of the field are subject to a centrifugal effect because those on the inside will push them wider. Even if there is a considerable run-in prior to the first turn, horses drawn in the outermost stalls must expend a lot of energy to cut across the field and negotiate a position close to the inside running-rail. The alternative is to miss the break and adopt a position at the rear of the field which may be highly disadvantageous in the latter stages of the race. The acuity (tightness) of the turns varies depending on the course and the distance of the race. This is one reason why the draw bias should be considered separately for each race distance run at a given course. For example, races over 7f at Ayr and 1m at Bath start from a chute that joins the main course like a tributary stream after 100 yards or so.

2) **Proximity to the running rail:** The running rail serves as a reference point and helps horses to keep in a straight line. On very wide courses such as the Rowley Mile at Newmarket, the field may bisect into two groups, one adhering to each rail. When horses remain in a single group that occupies the centre

of the course, those that are "covered up" in the heart of the field often gain an advantage over horses which are more exposed at the periphery of the group.

3) **The going:** The condition of the ground is seldom identical across the width of the track. When the going is soft, the strip along the inside rail may become muddier and more distressed after each race. This effect becomes progressively worse throughout the season. If the ground close to the inside rail becomes very sticky then the typical draw bias is often reversed because those runners on the outside of the field benefit from running on faster ground. For example, the artificial surface Fibresand (Southwell) wears easily and this has the effect of creating a slower strip of ground adjacent to the inside running-rail after successive races. For these reasons, the draw may also exert a greater effect in the last race of the day than it does in the first. The camber of the track (slope from one side to the other) and the drainage of the soil or artificial surface will affect the prevalence of slower patches of ground.

4) **Track husbandry:** The type of watering used on the course will exert a marked effect on the condition of the ground. For example, the seasoned race reader Alan Amies noted that the effects of the draw at Thirsk depend on whether the track has been watered or natural rainfall has occurred. This observation is probably also true of sprints at Catterick. **We are in an age when courses, although they may not admit it, actively manipulate their biases**. This is especially true on the artificial surfaces where attempts to eradicate the bias often end up completely reversing it. Added to this, biases often spring up on a meeting-by-meeting basis because of the harrowing or ploughing of the surface; procedures which don't take place evenly across the entire track.

5) **The size of the field:** The draw bias is partly determined by the size of the field. In a two-runner race, the horses concerned will be racing over practically the same ground whereas in a field of 25 runners, the two horses drawn at opposite ends of the starting stalls will effectively be running in different races. The conventional wisdom is that the draw bias is exaggerated by large fields and simply does not exist in small fields. Intuitively, this description sounds appealing but my research has forced me to question it.

6) **The distance of the race:** In general terms, the draw bias may exert a greater influence over shorter distances (under 1m) because there is less opportunity to recover from a weak start. However, there are plenty of biases over long distances that are caused by the shape of the course in question.

7) **The racing preferences of the horse:** Some horses are more likely than others to exploit a good draw and dispute the early lead whereas others produce their best performances when they are covered up and brought slowly into a race. A favourable draw would be wasted on a horse that prefers to race with the pack rather than at the head of affairs.

8) **Jockeyship:** An advantageous draw provides a jockey with an excellent hand, but he still has to play his cards right. There are many examples of jockeys switching sides to locate faster ground thus nullifying the draw's effects.

9) **The position of the stalls on the track:** At some racecourses, the starting stalls are occasionally moved to occupy different positions across the width of the track. Such alterations can completely reverse the effects of the draw. There are also times when a running rail will be moved in order to unveil a strip of

fresh ground. Unfortunately, not all such modifications are properly reported or recorded thus presenting a headache for most bettors but an opportunity for those organised enough to undertake detailed research and contact the racecourses in person.

The army of different factors listed above serves to create much confusion and pave the way for all sorts of mummery and piffle. It is inadvisable to provide prescriptive rules concerning the effects of the draw at a particular course due to the inherent variability of the bias. Those who make the attempt soon become lost in a forest of contradictions and caveats; their prescriptions are simply too labyrinthine to be of any practical use.

Interpreting the draw bias

How do you incorporate the effects of the draw into your betting decisions? A formbook might tell us that low-drawn runners often prevail at Chester. But what it is a low draw? Anyone would tell you that stall number one is low, but what about stall four in a ten-horse race? Do you still bet or do you keep your powder dry? This problem is exacerbated by the convention of trisecting the stall numbers into low-, middle-, and high-drawn runners. Such an approach leaves us with the following unacceptable scenario: the advice of the formbook is to back low-drawn horses in a particular race which happens to have nine runners. Therefore, if our selection is drawn in stall three, we conclude that the horse has a favourable draw and we make the bet. However, if the hypothetical steed starts from neighbouring stall number four, we consider the horse to be drawn in the "middle" and refrain from betting.

The draw bias simply does not operate in convenient geometric patterns. We cannot say that, as the stall numbers increase, so the advantage held by each successive runner will diminish in an incremental fashion. In fact, when a bias exists that favours low-drawn horses, it is quite normal for those runners drawn on the opposite flank to fare better than those drawn in the middle of the field. The runners that are housed in stalls one and two may have a fantastic record, whereas those situated in stalls three and four may fare very poorly because they are impeded by the horses drawn immediately inside them.

What is needed from a bettor's point of view is a method of quantifying the draw bias stall by stall; preferably presented in a graphical form for ease of comprehension. Several services and organisations have attempted to produce charts which visualise the draw's effects (for example, the charts at flatstats.co.uk or drawbias.com) but nothing yet has quite hit the mark. Cue an enterprising individual. Finally, the draw bias is an area of study which benefits massively from watching races in order to see how the bias influences the shape of the race. In many cases, the cold stats don't tell the whole tale.

The accumulative effects of the draw

A sophisticated angle is to locate runners whose form is over-rated because they were flattered by a good draw on a previous outing. Runners that have been impeded by a poor draw and yet have still run creditably are of even greater interest. In such instances, there is a genuine possibility that the betting public might collectively underestimate the relevant form and allow a runner to start at an inflated price. The draw bias causes all sorts of patterns. For example, a trend has emerged recently whereby horses are being "tactically" withdrawn from perceived poor draws (e.g. high stalls at Chester), going on to win well next time out.

The reporting of stall numbers

From 30 March 2011, starting stalls at racecourses classified as right-handed tracks were renumbered in ascending order from *right to left* (from the perspective of jockeys awaiting the start). Previously, starting stalls at all tracks were numbered from left to right. In line with other racing nations, stall number "1" will now always be adjacent to the inside rail. The change in practice is effective for all races, including those run on a straight course. Courses affected include: Ascot, Beverley, Carlisle, Folkestone, Goodwood, Hamilton, Kempton, Leicester, Musselburgh, Newmarket Rowley Mile and July Courses, Ripon, Salisbury, Sandown, and Windsor.

Class
The differing levels of competition

When evaluating the performance of a horse, it is essential to consider the strength of the opposition that it faced. The different strata of races displayed in Tables 1 and 2 provide a framework whereby horses can compete with runners of similar ability. The resultant hierarchy resembles the different divisions of the football league; I would not back the winner of a Class 5 selling race to beat the winner of the Epsom Derby for the same reason that I would not back a non-league football team to beat the Premiership champions. Both teams may excel in their given stratum of competition, but the Premiership team would have more *class*, a word which simply denotes a higher level of ability.

A seasoned approach to understanding the differences in class is to use race times. This allows us to assess, for example, how much faster a Group 1 winner is than a Listed winner (around 0.13 seconds faster per furlong at the latest count, which is a little under a length). What we find is that prize money correlates very well with speed. In other words, the bigger the prize money for first place, the faster the race is run, which makes sense doesn't it? In National Hunt racing, the best novices produce the fastest times, whereas in flat racing the maturation of juveniles is clearly discernible across their first and second seasons.

Moving up or down in class

Many betting approaches are built upon the concept of following horses that are migrating up or down in class. The seasoned perspective is that horses which are descending in class form the more favourable betting propositions because they merely have to reproduce the level of ability they have already shown in order to be competitive; runners that are rising in class must improve. Furthermore, a horse that has finished down the field in a valuable event may have been tailed off by its jockey when its chance had gone. If such a horse were entered into a weaker event in which it could compete, one might expect the animal to produce a faster run.

Class pars

An American technique which has gathered ground in the UK over recent years is that of assigning *class pars*. This is a selection method which essentially seeks to answer the question "what level of ability would a horse need to have demonstrated in order for it to be good enough to win a race of this class?" The way this question is answered is by setting "class pars" for every stratum of race. In many cases, these are assigned on the basis of a speed or handicap rating. Naturally, there is a lot more to it than that, but that's the gist. Some exponents allow their ratings to be heavily swayed by the *racecourse* at which a certain performance was recorded. This taps into an old belief that, among races of an apparently similar level of class and prize money, ones held at elite tracks such as Newmarket, Ascot, and Newbury represent much stronger form. This is an interesting concept as it may well hinge not just on the merit of the performances themselves, but on the *perceptions* of punters about the value of those performances. We also have the problem that "glamorous" courses like Epsom and York do stage some fairly humdrum meetings, the performances emanating from which are apt to be given too much respect.

Jumping

Over obstacles, the superior jumpers invariably beat the fastest runners. From a physiological point of view, the endurance needed to cover distances of two miles or more and the power needed to jump fences require very different types of fitness. Indeed, the genetic profiles of the best jumpers are similar to those of sprinters on the flat. Even Red Rum himself was bred as a sprinter! The key concept to understand when considering the effect of jumping on performance is *momentum*. If you have ever watched athletics on television then you have probably heard David Coleman or Colin Jackson elaborating on the importance of "getting that trail leg down with a snap". Some momentum will always be lost at the obstacle, but the best in the world become so by reducing this effect.

Gloria Victis, jumping like the proverbial stag

The real problem caused by a loss of momentum is that a runner is required to accelerate and thus waste energy. To make matters worse, inexpert jumpers often check their strides and decelerate into obstacles, which exacerbates the energy cost of the whole endeavour. Good jumpers must possess explosive strength, but above all they should be fluid and thus able to accommodate obstacles at speed. Jockeyship is of more importance in National Hunt racing than on the flat because the balance, strength, and skill of the rider can make a huge difference to the accuracy of their mount's jumping. It is important to recognise that steeplechase fences are not merely larger versions of hurdles. Whereas hurdles can be brushed through, fences must be *cleared*; the technique required is very different and much more demanding. Just as you should be wary of horses making their hurdling debuts, you should also be apprehensive of an animal that is stepping up from hurdles to fences. When the horse is thrown in *under race conditions*, you won't know whether it will sink or swim.

National Hunt racing in 2012 – a matter of life and death?

The health of flat racing's poor relative has become quite a popular topic, not least because the political climate regarding animal welfare is changing. There have long been undercurrents of protest that find their focus in the Grand National. These came to a head in 2011 when the great showcase made the news for all the wrong reasons. As someone who profits from betting on the results of jumps races, it's hard to ignore the dangerous reality that horses and jockeys face. Fortunately, initiatives in veterinary research, such as the programme at the University of Liverpool, are exploring ways in which fractures can be prevented. The BHA's new prescriptions for safe going are also a move in the right direction. In my own opinion, the collective benefits to humans and horses that are derived from racing do outweigh the health risks that are taken by jockeys and their mounts, but those risks need to be better acknowledged and more comprehensively addressed. Jump racing is, by its nature, a sport of life and death.

Part 3: Profitable Trends

Preface

Before I break from the stalls, I would just like to sketch out some background for this part of the book. You might wonder where I picked up all the ideas I have tested. Some of them are my brainchild, but others have been suggested to me by race readers and handicappers. Still more have come to me by virtue of fellow gamblers I chat with in forums and the suggestions of friends. On occasion, I have extrapolated an idea from another author, in which case I have credited it as such.

The statistics I have used are very elementary: the **strike rate**, which refers to the number of races won as a percentage, and the **profit per £1 staked**. As the strike rate relates to *performance*, we can use the data to answer questions along the lines of "do horses stepping up in distance to one mile *perform* better than those stepping down to one mile". If the performance is equivalent but we make much more money backing the latter group then we have uncovered clear evidence of under-betting. It is always valuable to know whether our selections are *performing* better than the alternatives or whether they are underestimated by the betting public and are therefore profitable to back.

To compare the profit statistic to a *return on investment* is slightly misleading because it arises from a series of small stakes. To say "I made 10p per £1 staked" is not the same thing as making 10% on a stock market investment. When betting, the maximum amount staked *at any point* might be less than even a $1/1000$ of the overall investment. Yet, as the results take place in a chaotic sequence, we would see large fluctuations in profit depending on exactly **when** we stopped that sequence. In the same way, if we were to stop a game of poker we would see dramatically different outcomes according to the hand which we chose to stop. So that's why a straight comparison with the return from an investment product can be a little misleading. All of the above depends very much on the *prices* we are taking about our selections. If we are dealing in longshots, then we need to be extremely cautious. If on the other hand, our game is to lay odds-on favourites then there is a lot less potential fluctuation in overall profit. For this reason, it is a fallacy to directly compare returns from laying and back approaches. If the prices about our selections are equivalent, then the *stake money* is going to be much higher (relatively speaking) when *laying*. This means that the level of profit will *appear* far less, although it should prove more reliable.

As is my custom, I have in some instances taken the liberty of reporting the overall profit returned when all the selections are backed with a £100 stake. I hope that this information will provide a more tangible representation of the amount that might have been won in a series of real bets. In these instances, I have rounded the overall profit to the nearest £100.

Prices used

All the profit figures that follow are based on SP returns. In practice, these numbers can be comprehensively beaten with expeditious betting, especially for selections starting at double-figure prices. So the SP statistics I used have two advantages: conservatism and objectivity. We *know* that we could have struck bets at these odds, and the systems tested in this way are therefore more likely to be sound. When it comes to laying prices, I use a formula based on the SP, which I have tested on the results of thousands of races (comparing actual *Betfair* prices with SPs). It is extremely conservative and also takes into account the payment of five per cent commission on the exchanges. So, my profit figures for laying approaches would be very readily beaten in a real series of bets. For this reason, I get justifiably excited when I uncover profit levels such as 15p per £1 staked – I know from experience that these are a lot more robust than they immediately appear.

Samples used

The samples that I have used consisted of flat races (turf and all-weather) run between March 2008 and July 2011 and National Hunt races run between April 2008 until June 2011. On occasion, I have used a five-year sample, but the general premise has been to use a sample covering the last three years, which was when my last book was published. I could have analysed every conceivable question separately for flat and jumps races, but this would have resulted in a report that was tedious in the extreme. So I have aimed to use either a flat or jumps sample to answer every question that I encountered.

The Market

Are the SP percentages in Ireland terrible?

Yes they are. I divided up SP percentages into seven different bands (under 100%, 100-105%, 105-110%, 110-120%, 120-130%, 130-140%, and over 140%). Figure 6 shows an Anglo-Irish comparison of the distribution of races within each of these bands. I would suggest the reason for the discrepancy is that the Irish betting market is more concerned with the impact of inside information that its GB equivalent. This leads Irish on-course and high street bookmakers to take a very conservative approach. You won't find many 100/1 shots flying in over the Irish sea, because they're all 20/1 tops! I'm exaggerating of course, but it is this conservatism coupled with a failure to embrace online betting which has left punters using Irish bookmakers with a poor deal.

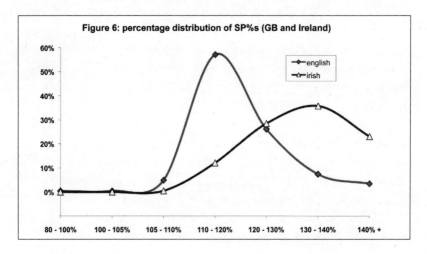

Figure 6: percentage distribution of SP%s (GB and Ireland)

Are favourites less reliable on artificial surfaces? (Flat)

There is a small difference. If we had backed every favourite on the turf we would lose 6p for every £1 staked, on all-weather tracks the return is a 12p loss. When field sizes have been accounted for, the strike rate percentages are similar.

Are beaten favourites worth following? (Flat)

Yes and no, it depends where they finished. To answer this question, I took my flat sample and focussed on horses that had returned odds-on for their last race. Odds-on favourites that were beaten but still *placed* actually fared well on their following start, they almost broke even. In fact, those starting their next races at less than 4/1 returned a small profit. Horses that were sent off at less than evens on their last start yet were unplaced proved profitable to lay in their following race, albeit with a small sample size.

In three-horse races is it *really* profitable to back the outsider? (Flat)

Amazingly – yes, under certain circumstances. If we ignore outsiders in single figures then the remaining long-shots show a massive profit of over £1 per £1 staked. A ready retirement plan? Not quite, there were only 50 qualifiers! But it is certainly not possible to *dismiss* the proposition based on those results. What we can be confident of is that odds-on favourites make for very poor value in these contests. There were 90 such runners in the sample, of which only 43% won their races, producing a profit of 20p per £1 risked when laid.

Does the SP on the previous start matter? (Flat)

Yes. The best option I found was to lay odds-on favourites that had started at 16/1 or greater on their most recent start. There were 138 which yielded a profit of £1,100 if laid to £100 backers' stakes each time. This result was regardless of where the runners in question had actually placed on their previous outings.

Ability Ratings

A quick note on the way I use these ratings throughout Part 3. In many cases, I want to highlight a particular trend by narrowing down the sample to horses *which have got a chance on form*. So in these instances I often use the top-rated runner in the race as a shorthand for the best form selection. When, I refer to the top-rated runner I am using the **Raceform** private handicap ratings rather than *Postmark*.

How well do ability ratings predict performance and profit? (Jumps)

Extremely well indeed. Figure 7 displays the relationship between Raceform's ability rating, profit, and performance for chasers running in stakes races. As we can see, the better-rated horses in each race not only perform very well but are extremely backable. Also we get a good idea, based on the chart, of how easy it is to dismiss certain runners by virtue of a low rating.

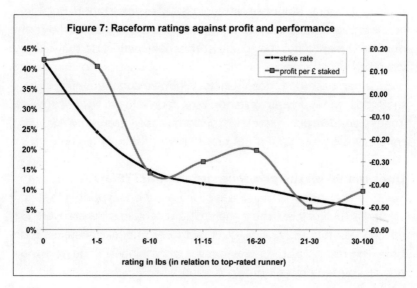

What is the best way to develop ability ratings?

As I have reported in the past, there is very little to be gained from constructing a rating which is based on an "average" of several recent runs or even the **best** amongst these runs. In fact, mean averaging tends to "dilute" the ratings making them far less potent whereas focussing on the best of several recent attempts tends to make the ratings less reliable. All of which goes to show the value of recent form and the folly of overestimating an animal's ability to recapture its best form. Handicap races are a very different story of course.

Are ratings equally accurate for all race distances? (Jumps)

No, not at all. This was an accidental discovery. I had intended to examine the performance of top-rated runners at different times of the year and instead entered the distance variable by mistake. What I noticed was that the ratings performed incredibly well for **chasers** running at distances of around 2m, 2m4f-2m6f, and 3m. Outside of these trips, which represent the standard "short", "mid", and "staying" divisions, the top-rated runners performed very badly. This finding hints that the accuracy of the ratings is being distorted by the failure of horses to get the specialist trips in question, be they long-distance slogs or the quirkier intermediate distances. For hurdlers, a slightly different picture emerged wherein the ratings performed well in staying events, and at around 2m2f. However, elsewhere, and particularly around the tricky 2m4f distance, top-rated runners actually made good laying fodder, which is a staggering trend.

Do top-rated horses perform better over certain distances? (Flat)

Yes, very much so. As you can see from Figure 8 overleaf, there appear to be two "hot spots": around 7f and the middle-distances. Sprint races, which are typically thought to be more opaque from the backer's point of view, seem to represent a corresponding "flat spot".

Do ability ratings predict profit better for juveniles? (Flat)

No. In fact the profit returned from backing top-rated runners is actually superior when we look at races for older horses. This may be because the ratings fail to adequately take into account the *improvement* of younger horses.

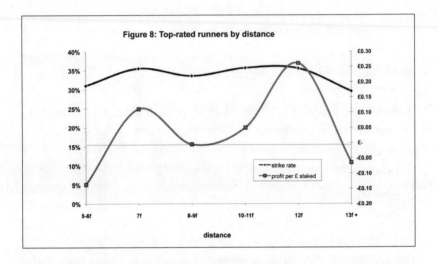

When it comes to top-rated horses, is there a difference in the profit returned depending on SP? (Flat)

Yes, very much so. Intuition would tell us that fancied top-rated animals should prove to be the best betting vehicles. But this is not the case at all. In fact, highly-rated runners who are somewhat overlooked in the betting market return a handsome profit whereas favoured runners return a loss. In fact, laying the 361 top-rated runners in the sample for backers' stakes of £100 each time resulted in a modest profit of £1,700 (strike rate of 44.3%). The most profitable runners to oppose are the in the 1/2 – 4/5 bracket. There were 150 of those and if you had laid them for backers' stakes of £100 then a profit of £2,300 would have followed.

How do top-rated runners perform in different field sizes? (Flat)

Much better in medium-sized fields (see Figure 10). It appears that small fields produce falsely run races that don't necessarily reflect form. On the other hand, large fields seem to promote chaos. This result ties in with my findings from the past. For example there

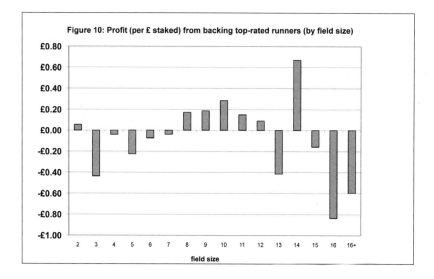

Figure 10: Profit (per £ staked) from backing top-rated runners (by field size)

is always money to be made laying odds-on favourites in large, competitive fields, rare though they are.

Does the openness of a race affect the returns derived from backing a top-rated horse? (Flat)

Yes it does. In my first test (see Figure 11), I have used the price of the favourite as an indication of how open the race is. Of course, this has its flaws: the price of the favourite is related to field size and it doesn't tell us if there is another horse very close to the favourite in the betting market. These concerns aside, we have a very strong trend in that top-rated animals produce profit in open races. In Figure 12 I have used a different variable to account for openness – the number of runners with single figure SPs. Nevertheless, I have arrived at the same conclusion as the first test.

Is there a limit to the amount of improvement that can be made in one season? (Flat)

I often watch progressive horses and wonder whether there is a limit

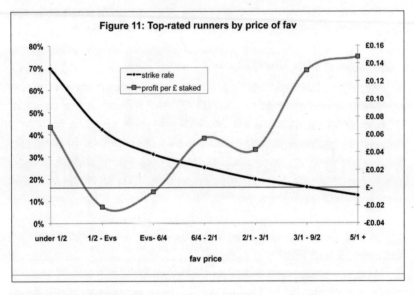

Figure 11: Top-rated runners by price of fav

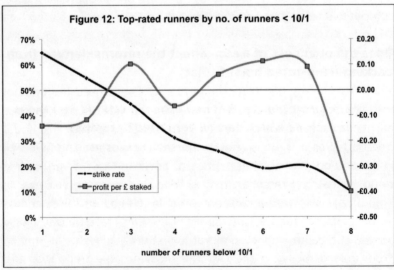

Figure 12: Top-rated runners by no. of runners < 10/1

to their improvement over the course of a season; a point at which they've hit an improvement "ceiling" and would therefore represent poor value. To test this idea, I created a variable which reflected the improvement shown between the start of the season and the race prior to the current outing. To render the calculations more effective I chose the best of the first two runs in the season as the baseline. The results surprised me a little. Two-year-olds are able to bear *a lot* of improvement during a season. Even horses that had already improved over 50lb made good betting propositions. In fact, betting on *any* animal which had already improved 15lb or more from the baseline produced good returns. There were 602 in my sample and the profit level was an acceptable 12p per £1 staked. From this 602, By far the best returns came from the group which had improved between 15 and 25lbs.

Three-year-olds were a different story entirely; the trends weren't clear at all. But, when I focussed on Class 1 races, a strong pattern emerged. Horses that had improved during the season to the tune of up to 10lb did very well indeed, both in terms of strike rate (18%) and profit (40p per £1 staked), above this "ceiling" of 10lb, profit and performance dropped off.

Are there discrepancies between the GB ratings and those of other nations which can be exploited? (Jumps)

Yes. Sam Walker, a ratings man at the *Racing Post* gave me this idea. A lot of work has gone into getting the *Postmark* ratings for Irish jumps races up to the same level as their UK counterparts. However, the official BHA ratings are compiled differently and horses have to be "re-rated" before crossing the Irish Sea to race on our shores. To get the ball rolling, I looked at the performances of all runners from Ireland racing in the UK. The most notable trend was that those under 2/1 were excellent laying fodder. Next, I incorporated the ratings angle and found that animals rated within 10lb of the top-rated runner were highly profitable to follow. I found 356 in my sample, to have backed them all with £100 stakes would have netted £9,100 profit (26p per £1 staked). This applied to hurdles **and** chases, stakes **and** handicaps. While the results lend credence to the suggestion that Irish runners are "under-rated" when transferring to Great Britain, there appears, to be another, even stronger trend at stake: they are underbet. Just about the most profitable subsample I found was that of Irish horses running in Stakes races in Ireland followed by a run in a British handicap. Those rated within 10lb of the top-rated runner were highly profitable to follow, all of which underlines the strength of the *Postmark* ratings when dealing with Irish jumpers (at the Cheltenham and Aintree festivals for example).

Speed
Is there a way to profit from speed without using ratings? (Flat)

Unquestionably, there are successful ways of using the "raw" data of race times. An example I gave in Part 2 involved directly comparing runners that have recently raced over the same course, trip, and ground (a surprisingly common occurrence). We can also get some mileage from the components of other compilers speed ratings. In the *Raceform* database, information is carried on the extent to which each race time differs from the respective median time (in seconds per mile). I decided to focus on this variable using a sample of stakes races. A smooth trend did not emerge until I looked at the runners that were at least two seconds (per mile) faster than the median time. Backing these 439 qualifiers on their next starts led to a reliable profit of £3,000.

Handicaps
Is it profitable to follow horses entering handicap company for the first time? (Flat)

Generally, no. There is an interaction with age here in that, the older the entrant, the poorer the returns. If we simply laid every runner over the age of three entering handicap company for £100 backers' stakes we would have made a profit of £27,100 from 415 bets. There is also a trend we can exploit for backing profit: Whereas runners entering three-year-old handicaps produced an abysmal return when backed blind (-39p per pound staked), three-year-olds that enter **three-year-old plus** handicaps do much better, presumably because of the large weight advantage they enjoy, leniency on the part of the handicapper in some cases, and a prejudice discounting their chances. I found 189 such runners, and while there was only an 11.2% strike rate, they returned a healthy profit of 28p per pound staked.

Does it pay to follow handicappers that are racing off a lower mark than they've won off? (Flat)

To examine this principle, I created a statistic to express where each runner stood in relation to a handicap mark it had previously won off. I pre-selected handicappers with a win in their last 15 starts. I then took the mark they had won off and subtracted their current mark. So a horse with a score of 10 would be running off a mark 10lb lower than its winning mark. Conversely, a runner with the score of -20 would be running off a mark 20lb higher than its winning mark. I found 277 runners with a score of 15 or more, meaning they were running at a mark much lower than they had previously won off. Backing all of these with £100 stakes generated a profit of £10,500. Next, I narrowed down my sample by excluding runners with an SP in double figures. My aim was to lay the runners which were racing off a much higher mark than they had previously won off, while retaining a sufficient sample size. I found 163 runners with a score of -15 or less. Laying each of these for backers' stakes of £100 resulted in a profit of £7,600.

When does it pay to back handicappers on the downgrade? (Jumps)

As we know, horses will descend the handicap slowly until such a point that they become profitable to back. Trying to anticipate this return to form is quite an art. While simply following horses that are racing off a considerably lower mark than the peak of their form might not lead to riches, there are some circumstances we can latch on to. For example, I found 159 **favourites** that were racing off a mark *at least 15lbs lower* than a peak they had achieved within the last ten runs. To have backed all of these to the tune of £100 would have yielded £3,500 (22p per £1 staked). That's a considerable profit bearing in mind the lack of value which favourites often represent. I extended the findings to horses starting at single figure prices and found that the same pattern of results held true.

How does weight carried affect performance in handicaps? (Flat)

Weight carried – which of course is a proxy for the relative handicap marks of the runners in the race – makes a substantial difference to performance. In fact, top-weighted runners win almost twice as often as bottom-weighted runners. This disparity holds true in races with both narrow (14lb) and wide (28lb) weight bands. However, the trend is almost perfectly accounted for in the prices on offer. I investigated several variables in relation to *weight carried* in order to see if there was an interaction effect. One of the most interesting was *race distance*. In wideband handicaps run over sprint distances, low-weighted runners seemed to be heavily underbet. In these instances, I found 488 qualifiers that had a weight advantage of at least 23lb (over the top-weight). To have staked £100 on all of these would have reaped a profit of £11,400. Surprisingly, the relationship between the weight-carried and the strike rate percentage broke down in longer distance races (>12f), to the extent that high-weighted and low-weighted runners won with similar regularity. Accordingly, there was a profit to be made from backing runners that benefited from a weight advantage of at least 23lb.

Does it pay to back horses carrying large weights over fences? (Jumps)

No. Perhaps because "backing topweights" is a rule commonly used in systems, this group of runners is overbet, especially those carrying 11st10lb or more and going off at less than even money. In contrast, there are some respectable profits to be had from backing lowly-weighted favourites (carrying no more than 10st), especially when they run on soft or heavy ground (in which case we're looking at around 30p per £1 profit). After researching various angles, I am of the tentative opinion that weight matters more in middle-distance handicaps (around 2m4f).

Are topweights or bottomweights systematically overbet? (Jumps)

Yes. Whereas topweights starting at less than 2/1 were good laying fodder (10p per £1 risked), backing bottomweights starting at 4/1 or less actually returned a small profit. So there is an inefficiency in the market; one which probably revolves around the old contention that a topweight is, after all, "the best horse in the race" according to the official ratings. In fact, topweights are often nominated as a selection rule in many of the poor systems which are pedalled on the internet. This might be why they are overbet.

Do handicappers on the upgrade make sound betting propositions? (Jumps)

That's a cautious yes. I looked for handicappers which had produced their best run for at least 15 outings on their previous start. While these animals did not perform any better than the average runner, when they were heavily supported (under 2/1 but especially when they were odds on) they were highly profitable to follow. From a small sample of odds-on favourites that qualified I found a profit of 18p per £1 staked. That's an unusually high figure for odds-on shots.

What we can certainly say is that these are the types of favourites we should be careful about opposing.

Does it pay to support handicappers bearing a win penalty? (Flat)

No. They return a small loss of around 7p per £1 staked.

How do maidens fare when moving into handicap company? (Flat)

Not well. The 122 in my sample produced a profit of 14p per £1 risked when laid. The one exception to this rule, which has been flagged up in the racing media, is when maidens enter into handicaps at around the distance of one mile. Sprinters are especially profitable to lay under these circumstances. Looking at my sample, we can include horses starting at 2/1 or less and that leaves us with 132 qualifiers, which if laid to £100 backers' stakes each time would have returned a profit of £3,100.

How do horses with selling form fare in handicap company? (Jumps)

Very well. It is all too easy for us to dismiss selling form when assessing a handicap race, especially if a horse is moving directly from selling to handicap company. I located runners in handicaps whose most recent run was in a seller. The trend I uncovered was that horses which had *won* a seller on their previous start represented excellent value. I found 232 runners of which 38 won (16.38 per cent). To have backed all of these to £100 stakes would have generated over £5,000 in profit (23p per £1 staked). This suggests that selling form may be underbet in handicaps to some extent.

Going
Can the published going reports be used to build an accurate portrait of a horse's going preferences

No. Going reports are simply not reliable enough to form the basis of this type of analysis. I have attempted to craft many systems on the principle that some individuals prefer softer ground, and while it is patently the case that they *do*, it is not discernible using the *formbook* data. I tried myriad alternatives, mostly based around the idea of finding horses that had repeatedly failed on soft ground (by virtue of placings or ratings). However, none of these bore fruit. Worse still, the *opposite* trend was given to appear wherein horses that had failed multiple times on soft going were profitable to back when they encountered that ground.

Sex
How does the performance of females differ across the season? (Flat)

As we can see in Figure 13, top-rated fillies perform better when in-season. They prove profitable to follow until mid-summer (25p per

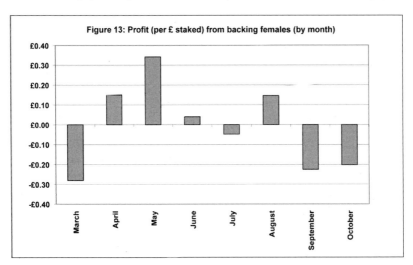

Figure 13: Profit (per £ staked) from backing females (by month)

£1 staked) and then profitable to lay as they come out of season in September, October, and November. This goes to show that simplistic statements such as "never back fillies against colts" can't be taken at face value. We have to ask when that filly is running.

Can we cash in by opposing mares over fences? (Jumps)

Yes. Here we are met with a situation very different to the flat. When jumping mares come into season during the spring their form dips alarmingly. Backing every qualifier in my sample during the month of February actually yielded a smart profit (15p per £1 staked from 252 runners). Gold is quickly transmuted back into lead though; looking at the 651 runners in March and April I found a catastrophic loss of 51p (per £1 staked). Indeed, they made acceptable laying fodder. Incidentally, a different picture emerges if we look at hurdlers. Much like their flat cousins, mares over the gentler obstacles are in profit from February to May! To focus this trend on profit I looked at favourites and found 327 qualifiers, £100 bet on all of them returned £5,500.

How does gelding affect a horse (except the obvious)? (Flat)

The first thing to say is that there is clearly a large break from racing involved, typically over a year, and this break doubtless has its own effects. When we look at new geldings running in stakes races there are no trends to report, apart from a good profit to be made from laying odds-on qualifiers. They are quite thin on the ground so it is worth widening the bracket to include those geldings at 2/1 and under, as these runners still return a good profit when laid. Another approach I used to increase the sample size was to include the second run post-gelding. These runners are also seriously worth opposing. When we turn to handicaps there are some very exciting bets at longer odds, new geldings starting at double figures and upwards show some fantastic profits (a profit of 40p per £1 staked from nearly 250 qualifiers in the 10/1-33/1 bracket).

Is the "big-race trends" angle as profitable to follow as it seems?

This question is almost unavoidable. The more seriously you bet, the more significant the big meetings will be to you; they are the cornerstones of the betting year. The intuitive logic of applying ten-year trends is almost inescapable: the most valued prizes in racing create distinct patterns both in terms of the way trainers prepare their charges and the types of animals which can succeed.

However, in betting, anything that seems like a panacea is in fact a little bit dangerous. I learned this the hard way. Probably the worst 18 months or so in my own betting records came from relying too heavily on big-race trends. There is something very appealing about them as a tool for finding value. For example, you might look at a big handicap and see that eight out of the last ten winners were carrying 11 stone or more and that runners over seven years of age have a terrible record. Suddenly, you have narrowed down a field of 23 to a manageable six. You might even want to back all of these against the field, quite literally backing the trend itself. Surely it's hard to lose with a Bowie-knife like this at your disposal? The truth is so very different. What you find is more like this: "five-year-olds have won this for the last six seasons" so you focus on those and then an eight-year old pops up, or maybe "champion hurdle seconds have been turned over in this every time they've attempted it, most of them at odds-on". . . but one goes in today.

The trends give you a blinkered view and a sense of false confidence. The reason for this is that:

1) **They are based on a minute sample size.** One result can throw the entire sample.

2) **They focus on winners rather than performance in a general sense.** Remember the trend that heavyweights couldn't win the Grand National? This pattern has been comprehensively overturned in recent seasons. In fact, shrewdies had been pointing out for a year or two before the turn in results that

heavily-weighted runners were filling the places so clearly could not be at too much of a disadvantage. Incisive betting commentators have been suggesting that a more sophisticated approach needs to be taken when considering big-race trends. The "percentage of runners beaten" statistic has been touted as it gives us a truer estimation of how a given variable (age, for example) impacts upon the performance of *every runner.*

3) **Trends are often presented in a misleading way.** It's one thing to say Irish horses have failed in this race – but what if they have only made up seven per cent of the runners? This is another issue that stems from a small sample size. In order to properly dismiss the chances of Irish runners in the example above, you would need to use a sample of hundreds of races – not just ten.

4) **A ten-year moving average is often too long a period.** The underlying trends are in fact more fluid and may shift every couple of seasons. Take, for example, the recent improvement in form shown by younger French-bred chasers which has resulted in a change to the weight-for-age allowances. What happened five years ago may be irrelevant now or even misleading.

5) **Trends are open to completely opposite interpretations.** I used to read the trends associated with Cheltenham Festival races and then form my own views based on them, only to find that the pundit whose article I was reading had reached a completely different conclusion because he had a different concept of what trends mattered the most.

6) **Trends are too exclusive if taken literally.** The Cheltenham Gold Cup is a good example of this limitation. Quite often we are left with a scenario whereby **no** horse can win according to the trends. And yet, surprisingly enough, a horse *does* win! Seemingly bombproof trends are overturned with great regularity.

So, what strategies can we use to overcome these drawbacks? To increase the sample size we need to include all runners (not just winners) but this has the effect of focussing our results on *performance* rather than *profit*, which is a counterproductive measure. One solution would be to conglomerate different races together and see if there was a super-trend that applies across the board. I attempted this with the Cheltenham Festival races.

Clearly, each contest has its own unique requirements, so many of the variables at our disposal would be useless. Age for example is highly specific to each race: the Champion Bumper, Champion Hurdle, Gold Cup, and Foxhunter Chase have their own patterns pertaining to the age of potential victors. Having said this, I have often wondered whether certain races might be grouped together – the championship chases for example, or the novice events. On this occasion however, I was looking for a variable which transcended the characteristics of each individual race and captured something specific about the *fixture* as a whole. At the Cheltenham Festival, the importance of previous course form, and in particular **festival form**, is often being trumpeted. So I decided to investigate this variable.

To concentrate on animals with a strong chance of victory I used performance ratings, choosing those within 10lb of the top-rated specimen in each race. I then selected qualifiers that had been *placed* over course and distance within the last 15 runs (I used placed efforts rather than wins so as to increase the sample size). A clear trend emerged. In simple terms, the more fancied runners (under 4/1) were very opposable whereas those starting at longer odds produced extremely high profits (£1.21 per £1 staked). Notably, these profits were considerably diminished by focussing only on horses that had previously been placed at Cheltenham (but not necessarily over the same distance). Another "global" trends variable I had some success with was the number of times a horse had been placed in Class 1 events. I feel that having the class to compete at the highest level is prerequisite to success in almost all of the festival races.

Cheltenham

Form

Does a winner's margin of victory in the previous race have a bearing on profit? (Flat)

Yes, an interesting minor trend emerged whereby there was an optimum margin of between two to three lengths which led to profit. This held for both stakes races and handicaps. Notably, both narrow-margin (< 0.5 lengths) and wide-margin (>9 length) victors produced terrible returns when backed. Indeed, wide-margin victors proved profitable to lay, presumably because of overbetting. The strike-rate trend differed between handicaps and stakes races. In the case of stakes races, the two to three length winners proved the best performers, whereas with handicaps, the wider the margin of victory, the better the subsequent strike rate.

Does the margin of defeat in the last race have a bearing on profit? (Flat)

No. I found that the margin of defeat was totally irrelevant in handicaps. In stakes races, the further a horse was beaten by last time, the poorer it performed on its subsequent start. But this trend is entirely accounted for in the prices on offer.

Is selling form especially relevant when betting in sellers? (Jumps)

Yes. Just as mountains like Ben Nevis have their own "microclimate" which may not follow the weather patterns of the surrounding area, specialist races have their own form book. In other words, when you are looking at a seller, give the strongest credence to form from other selling races. To examine this I looked at runners entering a seller directly from another selling race. **When supported** (under 2/1) these animals show a slight profit when backed. This profit is rendered more comfortable if we ignore animals that were unplaced last time out.

Is it profitable to follow horses that have come out of certain "key" races? (Jumps)

This is a system that's close to my heart. It's also as old as the hills. I remember Nick Mordin writing about it in the eighties when he relayed the idea of following every animal that had been in last season's Cheltenham Festival Champion Bumper. Of course, that system ceased to be profitable. In fact, it is now more likely you'll profit from *laying* the qualifiers. Nevertheless, it got me thinking. What I like about the approach is that it "trumps" the market because a horse that is carrying some good form will *eventually* show it, even if it takes several opportunities. By this time the market would have given up on the animal and the price would represent value. In short, it's a good way to circumvent the simplistic attitudes of the crowd and tap into some real value. There are several striking patterns in evidence, some of which defy intuition. For example, until recently the winner of the Epsom Derby rarely won another race in his subsequent career, with many of those starts being at shorter odds. I know a smart football gambler who told me about a system that

Motivator. A colt who defied the trend of Derby winners subsequently underperforming

follows the same principle. What he told me was that every year there are a couple of mid-table teams that show a profit on the season if you simply back them in every match. They carried enough form to win a decent share of matches against low- and mid-table opposition whilst occasionally overturning a bigger team at long odds.

The same principle is at stake in the "ten to follow" competitions that exist in our sport. With all this in mind, I went back to basics and looked at some of the other Cheltenham Festival championship races and investigated what would happen if you backed the runners in question for their next five starts (I played around with a few variations on this theme first). What I found was that certain races, like the Gold Cup or the Champion Hurdle, are a little bit like jumps equivalents of the Derby. Runners that have passed through races like this can be successfully opposed, especially if they were placed in the key race. This may be because the form of these key events is over-rated; after all, the Gold Cup is simply a race like any other in which horses can have a good (or bad) day at the office.

Other races produced very different trends, for example there was a lot of profit to be made from following runners that had been through the Champion Chase or the Supreme Novices Hurdle. Clearly these races provide a springboard for future success rather than a peak which must ultimately be descended from. Races such as the Arkle and the Triumph Hurdle gave rise to some equivocal results with no clear pattern. There is definitely some real merit in this approach. One of the things I have picked up from skilled race readers is that each big meeting not only resolves tantalising form questions but also gives us some potent clues as to what's going to happen over the months and years to come.

Going
How do form-picks and market favourites fare under different going conditions? (Flat)

This is one of those "mighty oaks" that never seems to change. As a rule, fancied and top-rated horses do well on fast ground and badly on slow ground. Just looking at favourites, I found 86 running on heavy ground which returned an excellent laying profit of 11p per £1 risked. On the other hand, if you'd backed the 253 runners I found that were racing on firm ground to £100 stakes, a profit of £5,000 would have been your reward. As favourites don't generally show a profit (or get particularly close to showing a profit) that's a cracking result. I also conducted an analysis using top-rated runners. This time I used Going Stick readings to separate them. While the 167 qualifiers running on fast ground (=> 10 on the stick) produced a handsome profit of 25p per pound staked, those running on slower surfaces (for which I had to use the broad range of =< six) showed a loss.

Season
Do some horses peak at a certain time of the year? (Jumps)

Definitely. This is a question well suited to the jumping code as the protagonists build up their careers over several years, which should make seasonal patterns easy to spot. The way I isolated qualifiers was by looking for horses that had won at least twice during the month of the current race (twice before in March, for example). In stakes races, such runners did much better than the rest of the sample, but only returned a slight profit. The handicap qualifiers were a different story. There were some 260 of them in my sample, and backing each for £100 would have yielded a profit of almost £10,000 (the profit level being an other-worldly 36p per £1 staked).

Is there a particular period in each season when favourites show a profit? (Flat)

No. I found this trend altered year on year, which is unsurprising as it must be partly based on the weather. I used four years in my sample and there was no month in which a profit was made backing favourites in every year.

Fitness
Does the period of rest between runs affect performance and profit? (Flat)

Yes, although there is a clear difference between stakes and handicap races. In stakes races, the rest period makes no difference to either performance or profit, whereas in handicaps those returning after short breaks (<10 days) perform markedly better than other animals and those returning after long breaks (>300 days) markedly worse. Let us turn our attention to fancied runners, specifically favourites. What we find is that any runners returning within seven days are profitable to follow. This is one of those "mighty oak" trends that has not changed for decades. There is a whole clutch of systems built around this "boomerang" principle, so it's staggering that it still holds water. I found 1,021 favourites returning after a short absence. Backing all of them to the tune of £100 gave a modest profit of £3,000. This profit level rises considerably to 26p (per £1 staked) if we focus on top-rated horses instead of favourites.

Favourites returning after a long absence (>four months) were also profitable to follow in **handicaps**. The profit-per-£1-staked was 11p which may not sound vast, but it is considerable for favourites, which do not generally represent value. Such a finding perfectly demonstrates the nature of handicaps; in that form dating back many months can prove highly valid. It would be easy to suggest that this finding was simply due to handicappers turning out at the beginning of the season, but this was not the case. There was also money to be made by laying favourites that had been off course for between three and four months. This pattern held up well for both handicaps and stakes races.

I delved into the trends relating to rest periods a little further, and it seems that age plays a prominent role. If we go back to the boomerang system (returning within seven days) and look at ALL runners by age, an interesting fact emerges: Younger horses (two- and three-year-olds) are big losers on the book whereas older horses (four-year-olds and over) are big winners (22p per £1 staked).

Does exposure affect profit? (Flat)

Yes it does. For the purposes of this test I created a variable which accounts for the number of days a horse had taken to run six times (before today's race). For example, a horse that had been out six times inside two months is definitely overexposed whereas six runs in two years would probably indicate underexposure. If we look at all horses then there are no trends whatsoever. In fact, the data is a complete mess. But if we focus on top-rated runners in stakes races, then an interesting pattern emerges. Figure 14 demonstrates exactly the kind of smooth trend in profits that I seek. In this sample, if we had backed the underexposed runners (those that took at least 60 days to complete their last six runs) then a profit of £7,500 follows to £100 stakes (10p per £1 staked). By comparison, the overexposed runners showed quite a considerable loss. This demonstrates neatly

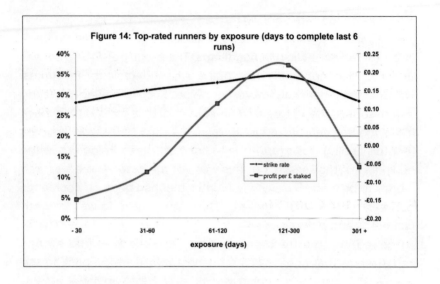

Figure 14: Top-rated runners by exposure (days to complete last 6 runs)

that punters following the form horse are failing to take into account the fact that all good runs come to an end.

Can horses bounce? (Flat)

This title refers to the proposition that horses put in a stinker after they've run well following a long absence. "Bouncing" is a pet theory of armchair punters and racing commentators the world over. For this test I've set the "long absence" to between five and eight months; I didn't want it to include horses returning from injuries, operations and suchlike. The trend I uncovered is markedly different for handicaps and stakes races. In the latter, horses that return to the racetrack quickly (boomerang) after the long absence do rather well. Backing each of the 614 qualifiers netted over £4,000 profit. With handicaps, there is an understandably different trend. Here we find that horses which remain off course for *at least two months* after their return from a long absence show a strong profit; there were 153 qualifiers, £100 staked on each yielded nearly £5,000.

I wondered whether distance might influence the degree to which a horse can bounce back so I looked at sprints (<=6f) and long distance races (>13f). In the case of the latter I saw a very strong profit trend favouring runners that remained off-track for at least two months following their return from a long absence. However, the sample size was far too low. Turning to sprinters, the trend strongly favoured those returning to the racetrack within a month. My sample contained 617 horses that had returned from a long absence and then ran again within a month. Backing all of these with £100 stakes would have netted a profit of £5,200.

Racereader Comments

Comments are widely available and would seem to hold the keys to profit because they represent an objective account of the "shape" each race took. It turns out that the information held in comments is significant, but not in the way we might expect. In fact, certain comments are inevitably associated with overbetting. **"Strongly"** is one such comment. The odds-on runners I found which finished or ran on "strongly" on their previous starts returned a huge loss. This may also have been because they were ambitiously entered into tough races. Subtler terms such as **"readily"** and **"gamely"** are associated with profit in subsequent races.

When considering comments, the key is to know which other variables to "cross" them with. For example, while runners earning the comment "readily" returned a comfortable profit when backed on their following starts, most of this profit was concentrated in upper-class races (Classes 1 and 2). In this restricted sample, the qualifiers returned 58p per £1 staked. Negative comments such as **"weakened"**, **"soon beaten"**, **"no extra"**, or **"never nearer"** show a predictable relationship with profit in that they create sound opportunities for laying odds-on shots. Horses that were not able to **"trouble"** the leader(s) are an interesting case. While this sounds like a negative it need not be. In fact, the comment might very well represent a solid second or third placing in a race. This is reflected in the fact that runners thus described show a large profit on their subsequent starts, especially when backed at longer odds (double figures).

Trainer
Can I make money by following certain trainers when the "price is right"? (Flat)

In the final edition of *Against the Odds*, I ran an analysis which highlighted certain trainers whose charges were very profitable to follow at short odds, but very costly to support at long odds. The disparity in profit according to SP was far greater than the favourite-longshot bias would lead us to expect. Interestingly, the analysis threw up the names of trainers who were associated with gambling activity, Barney Curley for example. In a sense, I was inferring that the sharp differences in profit were likely to have been caused by support for the runners from inside the stables in question. However, I didn't have at my disposal the data relating to the market moves, or indeed who was behind the moves, so it might equally have been the case that these trainers were very adept at placing their horses so as to maximise the chances of scoring a win. Some trainers are fantastic at finding bad races for their horses!

Trainer Ann Duffield

Since the recent global depression, many trainers have seen their strings reduced by half or more. In response, handlers such as Ann Duffield have reduced owners' fees in return for a greater share of the prize money. This provides an even bigger incentive for the trainer to produce winners of some description. For example, in 2009 Duffield managed 28 wins with a string of only 32 horses. Table 7 features an analysis of returns produced by backing runners sent off at prices under 4/1 and a corresponding figure for runners at prices greater than 4s.

TABLE 7: BACKING FLAT TRAINERS BY SP (FLAT RUNNERS)

Trainer	under 4/1			over 4/1		
	number	profit	per £ stkd	number	profit	per £ stkd
G M Lyons	200	£26.28	£0.13	935	-£261.00	-£0.28
Clive Brittain	136	£23.39	£0.17	961	-£165.50	-£0.17
T Stack	134	£20.85	£0.16	468	-£100.00	-£0.21
David Lanigan	72	£20.06	£0.28	247	-£67.50	-£0.27
Stuart Williams	193	£13.72	£0.07	757	-£379.50	-£0.50
Alan King	50	£13.52	£0.27	281	£31.50	£0.11
Patrick Martin	26	£12.66	£0.49	476	-£220.50	-£0.46
Derek Shaw	104	£12.01	£0.12	860	-£265.00	-£0.31
Barney Curley	27	£11.50	£0.43	113	-£33.00	-£0.29
Patrick Morris	53	£10.96	£0.21	616	-£275.00	-£0.45
Howard Johnson	74	£10.12	£0.14	357	-£128.50	-£0.36
Rae Guest	86	£9.57	£0.11	423	-£77.90	-£0.18
Malcolm Saunders	53	£9.02	£0.17	300	-£54.50	-£0.18
David O'Meara	78	£8.12	£0.10	192	-£54.50	-£0.28
Harry Dunlop	51	£7.36	£0.14	517	-£278.50	-£0.54

NB: £ stakes were used

Is it profitable to back horses following a change of trainer? (Flat)

In several previous analyses, I have shown that horses can display a sudden, unexpected upturn in form when running for a new trainer. The approach I used this time was to try and isolate the runners with a reasonable chance of victory, while retaining a workable sample size.

So I selected only runners rated within 5lb of the top-rated animal in the race. The trend I sought has definitely vanished in respect of the *first* run for the new trainer, so I decided to look at the second and third runs. The results were very promising although unexpected. Laying horses starting their second or third run for a new trainer led to a considerable profit. For runners priced under 2/1 there were 624 qualifiers and the profit was 13p per £1 risked, whereas if we focus on animals starting at evens or less then the number of qualifiers drops to 171 but the profit leaps up to 29p. This may be attributable to betting patterns or possibly even the process of acclimatising to a new yard; horses being very sensitive to their surroundings.

Is the idea of following certain trainers at festival meetings a good angle? (Jumps)

No, not as good an angle as many bettors think. Trainers do target specific fixtures, for example Martin Pipe used to have a stellar record in Cheltenham's Open meeting in November. However, the prices on offer will generally take these trends into account as they are well known. I looked at the data from several notable jumps meetings and found that, when I assessed results on a yearly basis, there were hardly any examples of consistent profit. The best outcome I found in relation to the Cheltenham Festival was Ferdy Murphy being in profit four years out of the last five.

Are there any other ways to pinpoint which trainers are on form coming into a festival meeting? (Jumps)

Having failed with the yearly trends (above) I sought other ways to capitalise on "hot" training performances in the all-important festival meetings which make up the nexus of the jumping season. The first approach I tried without success was to follow trainers that *had already turned out a winner in the said meeting;* for example, backing the trainer of the Champion Hurdle winner in all subsequent festival races. I tried a host of different angles without success so I moved on to look at the recent strike rate of the trainer, taking the Cheltenham Festival as an example. This too was disappointing so I trialled a slightly odd method, that of looking at the *profit* generated by backing a given trainer's runners in the preceding days. This produced some much more meaningful trends. I looked at various time periods ranging from 10 to 75 days and finally settled on 14 days as the ideal time frame. I found 145 festival runners trained by a handler whose runners were at least 50p in profit (per £1 staked) for the period of two weeks leading up to the festival. To back these with £100 stakes yielded a handsome £2,700 profit (19p per £1 staked).

What's the best way to capitalise on a trainer in form? (Jumps)

The trainer's recent record is a matter of hot debate and speculation in many betting forecasts. Various statistics abound, but are any of them useful? Conventional strike-rate statistics are often included in mathematical models of performance prediction, yet they are somewhat feeble in isolation. Arguably their best use comes with very specific racing populations (two-year-old maidens for example). I have used the variable of recent trainer profit to good effect in the past (the amount of profit derived from backing the trainer's runners over a specified recent period), so I examined the data a little more closely with this approach in mind. While I didn't uncover profit when looking at every runner *across the board*, we do find a trend if we focus only on favourites. In this case, trainers whose recent profit rate was above £2 (per £1 staked) sent off favourites which won over 42% of their races and showed a profit of 20p per £1 staked.

I increased the sample size by stretching the time frame to 30 days (from 14 days). What I found was that there may be some money to be made by backing longshots sent off by trainers in profit (>£1 profit per £1 staked). While the profit level from my 1,367 qualifiers was modest (6p per £1 staked), there would be great opportunities to increase this using *Betfair* or *Tote* odds as the bracket of prices I focussed on was 10/1 upwards. Another frequently discussed method is the *Racing Post*'s "run to form" statistic which assesses the percentage of a trainer's charges which are running up to their expected form level (as expressed by ability ratings). On the surface this would seem to be a highly sophisticated technique but I have found it to be of limited value, it certainly doesn't lead to any simple method for generating profit.

Traveller's Check (Flat)

This is a system that features in the *Racing Post*'s signposts section and appears to be built on a highly intuitive logic. Namely, the trainer wouldn't have bothered sending it all that way if it wasn't going to win. As with all such systems, there is an opposing school of thought, which Alan Potts neatly summarised as follows: "If it was any good he'd have run it at a decent course closer to home". In other words, the horse is only making the marathon journey because it would be unlikely to win anywhere else. These animals are certainly overbet as they stick out like a shark in a fishpond. The problem with this sort of analysis, if conducted on a trainer-by-trainer basis, is sample size. So I came up with the solution of lumping several Newmarket trainers together and seeing how their runners performed collectively when sent afar. I isolated the courses in the far north of the country (e.g., Yorkshire, Northumbria) and Scotland, excluded ones that host prestigious meetings and added one from the south (Brighton) and one from the west (Chepstow) which involved similarly long drives.

What I found was that horses sent on long trips from Newmarket were probably best laid, although runners at Catterick, Hamilton, and Newcastle rather spoilt the trend. The profit level was high (24p per £1 risked) but there were only 100 qualifiers so the jury is still very much out. A rule that is often touted and which I might have included is the one pertaining to the number of horses a trainer has sent to the meeting in question. There are also formulae which work out the cost of the journey (in diesel) against the prize on offer, which seems an ingenious approach. When all is considered, I think the "traveller's check" concept is overblown and I will not be returning to it again.

Is it possible to make money from the seasonal patterns trainers display? (Jumps)

Very much so. A good example of these patterns is the way that trainers handle their horses after a lay off. Let's say for the sake of argument that a lay off is a break of at least 150 days. As we can see in Table 8, trainers such as Nigel Twiston-Davies are celebrated for starting the season with a bang. Compare Twiston-Davies' runners with those of Philip Hobbs who has a quieter autumn but a much bolder spring with his returners. It helps us if we consider the market's view of the qualifying bets. For example, Howard Johnson's returners are good performers (21p per £1 staked, 176 qualifiers), but those that start at 4/1 or more especially so: I found 94 such beasts which, if backed with the customary £100 stakes would have yielded a profit in excess of £6,000.

TABLE 8: THE PERFORMANCE OF NIGEL TWISTON-DAVIES' AND PHILIP HOBBS' STRINGS AFTER A LAY OFF BY MONTH

	TWISTON-DAVIES			HOBBS		
Month	number	SR%	profit per £ stkd	number	SR%	profit per £ stkd
January	4	0%	-£1.00	15	33%	£2.43
February	11	18%	-£0.63	21	14%	£0.25
March	6	0%	-£1.00	15	13%	£0.40
April	3	0%	-£1.00	26	27%	£0.64
May	9	11%	-£0.33	9	11%	-£0.44
June	5	0%	-£1.00	4	0%	-£1.00
July	4	0%	-£1.00	9	0%	-£1.00
August	3	67%	£4.50	9	22%	-£0.51
September	25	20%	-£0.24	18	22%	-£0.29
October	60	22%	£0.40	135	17%	-£0.33
November	33	12%	-£0.28	121	15%	-£0.13
December	10	0%	-£1.00	35	11%	-£0.66

In what sorts of races is the trainer a key consideration? (Jumps)

Bumpers. Generally speaking, trainer statistics come into their own in races contested by unexposed juveniles. There are several equivalents on the flat; two-year-old maidens for example.

Here is a system called "bumper kings" that I read about in an article by Eamonn Hames in the *Irish Sun*: back any runner in an Irish National Hunt Flat race trained by either Michael Bowe, William Fitzpatrick, Nicky Henderson, Willie Mullins, Charles O'Brien, or Dermot Weld. The system had been in good profit over recent seasons so I sought to find out whether I could replicate the results with my own sample. The answer was a big "yes" as it turned out, from 381 qualifiers I had 122 winners and a 14p profit (per £1 staked). Notably, the profit shot up to 69p when I focused on the less-fancied selections (over 4/1), these runners clearly still benefited from the general principle of the system but represented even better value. Pleasingly, the profits were consistent over time (season-on-season) and continued *after* the article had been published – a key point. I extended the idea to English bumpers by checking to see the profit which could be obtained simply by following the handlers who I regarded as the leading two exponents: David Pipe and Nicky Henderson. This system showed an excellent overall profit. My disappointment at a slight loss over the first few months was assuaged by the consistent profits which flowed since the start of 2009.

The Bumper Kings. From left: Michael Bowe, Nicky Henderson, Willie Mullins, Charles O'Brien and Dermot Weld

Jockeys

Is it profitable to back handicappers benefiting from an apprentice allowance? (Flat)

No. In fact, when these runners are odds-on it's a great idea to lay them. I found 102 qualifiers which yielded a profit of £2,000 when laid to £100 backers' stakes. I think this result has more to do with the strategies of trainers than the skills of the jockeys concerned.

And what about in stakes races? (Flat)

In this case we find that, while it is still profitable to lay the mounts of apprentices when they are odds-on (to the tune of 10p per £1 risked), a slight profit is shown from backing all other qualifiers; nearly all of which is attributable to the 3lb claimers. This result certainly doesn't suggest the standard of apprentice riding is poor.

Are female jockeys underbet? (Flat)

Female jockeys used to be chronically underbet and thus represented excellent value; such was the myopic sexism of your average 1990s punter. I wondered if this had changed since the rise to power of female jocks over the past few years. After all, we're now rather used to seeing them win Group 1 races and storm the hill at Cheltenham in March, punching the air as they go. Rather oddly, the trend is now reversed in that, under certain circumstances, jockeys with two X-chromosomes seem to be overbet. I went through the records of the most prominent female jocks including some ascendant stars such as Julie Burke. What I found was that, when riding short-priced favourites, the women can be profitably opposed (I had to include runners as big as 2/1 to increase the sample size). Take Hayley Turner for example, her shorter-priced mounts profited 22p per every £1 risked when laid. It was the same for the others I tested with the one glaring exception of Milkshake. So, either the female jocks are overbet when they ride hot-pots or they aren't very good, in which case the dinosaurs from the 1990s were right all along. As ever, it's more the attitude of punters that shapes profit not the results themselves. In either case, I had an enjoyable afternoon doing this. It's such a shame that the formbook doesn't come with big pictures. Never mind, if I lay the female jocks enough, I'll have enough money to buy myself one of those lovely calendars.

Good laying propositions? From left: Hayley Turner, Kelly Harrison and Kirsty Milczarek

Are jockey-trainer combinations worth noting? (Jumps)

As I have written in the past, the jockey is one of the least serious considerations for successful backers. But there are a few exceptions to this rule and *rider bookings* is one of them. The success of a jockey when riding for the trainer who retains them is a reflection of the handler's own prowess and the horses in their yard. Nevertheless, the booking of a specific jockey can prove highly significant, not least because it reflects both the trainer's and the owner's view of its chances.

Table 9 contains a list of these profitable combinations in jumps racing. To hone in on profit, I included only runners in single figure odds, and only combinations with at least 30 runs during the period of the sample. Clearly, the vast majority of the profitable combinations are not partnerships between trainers and their first stable jockeys. There are a couple of exceptions, for example Barry

Geraghty's placing on the table is impressive considering the sheer volume of rides involved. Celebrated jockeys such as AP McCoy produce very different levels of profit depending on which trainer they ride for. For example, the "old school" combination of Pipe and McCoy clearly outstrips the intuitively appealing Nicholls McCoy partnership. The reason for this could well prove to be over-betting. Noel Fehily is relatively unusual in that he is moderately profitable to follow with two different trainers (Paul Nicholls and Jonjo O'Neill). To complete the analysis I separated the sample up by seasons to see how consistent the trends were over time. Barry Geraghty acquitted himself well again as did Richie McLernon riding for Jonjo O'Neill and Paul Townend riding for Willie Mullins.

TABLE 9: SUCCESSFUL TRAINER-JOCKEY COMBOS

Trainer	Jockey	number	profit	per £ staked
Howard Johnson	Paul Gallagher	41	£24.60	£0.60
Philip Hobbs	Giles Hawkins	39	£16.75	£0.43
W P Mullins	D J Casey	83	£30.47	£0.37
David Pipe	Hadden Frost	31	£9.83	£0.32
David Pipe	Danny Cook	76	£22.26	£0.29
W P Mullins	E Mullins	58	£16.33	£0.28
David Pipe	A P McCoy	59	£13.85	£0.23
David Pipe	Timmy Murphy	153	£32.70	£0.21
Paul Nicholls	Noel Fehily	42	£7.95	£0.19
Alan King	Jack Doyle	50	£9.45	£0.19
Alan King	Gerard Tumelty	78	£12.00	£0.15
Nicky Henderson	David Bass	76	£11.31	£0.15
Howard Johnson	Ryan Mania	42	£5.17	£0.12
Jonjo O'Neill	Noel Fehily	111	£13.19	£0.12
Nicky Henderson	Felix De Giles	113	£10.22	£0.09
W P Mullins	P Townend	290	£26.10	£0.09
Jonjo O'Neill	Richie McLernon	241	£19.58	£0.08
Nicky Henderson	Barry Geraghty	504	£36.20	£0.07
Howard Johnson	James O'Farrell	44	£3.08	£0.07
David Pipe	Johnny Farrelly	142	£9.51	£0.07
Paul Nicholls	R Walsh	674	£7.85	£0.01

Note: £1 stakes used

Richie McLernon

Are popular jockeys overbet? (Jumps)

Here is a great example of why it pays to oppose the crowd. To the uninitiated, backing AP McCoy blind in the best races might seem like a sure-fire money winner. In fact, the opposite is true. Whereas it doesn't pay to oppose McCoy-piloted favourites *generally*, if we do so in Class 1 and 2 events, the profits are considerable. I found 106 of these beasts, to have laid each to the tune of £100 would have left us with a £3,000 profit. Strangely, backing favs ridden by the great man in the *lowest* echelon of jumps racing – Class 6 – would have actually led to a profit. Of course, all of these are likely to have been in bumper races. I checked a few other candidates and, sure enough, both Robert Thornton and Ruby Walsh produced remarkably similar results. Not so Barry Geraghty or Richard Johnson who for some reason are dangerous to oppose when riding favourites in the better events. This is an opaque trend but intriguing nonetheless. Consider a direct comparison of Walsh and Geraghty in Class 1 races. During the course of my sample they both rode 233 qualifiers. In the case of Ruby, 58 won (25 per cent strike rate) returning a relatively small loss of £700 to £100 stakes. Compare that to Geraghty who rode 49 winners in the sample (21 per cent strike rate) yet returned a profit of £4,400.

The Draw
Can I make money backing the draw at Southwell?
It would be hard not to. In many ways Southwell is the ideal test bed for approaches built around the draw. The Fibresand surface is much looser than *Polytrack*, which makes acceleration hard and impedes those behind due to kickback. Added to this, the way the track is rolled appears to treat the centre twice which creates a faster strip. The upshot is that those drawn high when running on the round course (all races above 5f) can run the turns slightly wide and then adopt the quicker strip in the middle of the track during the run in. Or at least that's what the formbook said.

Backing the draw blind is a trifle haphazard, so I resolved to take a more scrutinous approach and select runners within 5lb of the top-rated animal in each race. I segmented the draw into pairs: stalls one and two, stalls three and four, the highest two stalls, and the two stalls immediately inside them. As expected the 5f straight course yielded a bias which favoured the inner stalls, with three and four getting by far the best of it. Over every other distance the bias favoured those on the outside in the manner described above. The results were so good that *both* pairs of outer stalls (the highest two and the two immediately inside them) showed a profit for each distance. **In total there were 429 qualifiers, £100 on each would have returned an eye-popping £36,300.** At this rate, Southwell could well usurp Cheltenham as my favourite racetrack.

Age
Are early foals more precocious? (Flat)

The story behind this nugget of an idea is that, although they may share a singular equine birthday, each year's crop of two-year-olds is actually foaled across several months. It is clear in Figure 15 that the performances of two-year-olds in the early part of the season bear a direct relationship with their foaling months; the older the animal, the more likely it is to win. However, this trend is not reflected in the market. To further investigate, I examined the profit that resulted from backing favourites according to their foaling month. This time I garnered findings that were more promising. Although I only found 41 favourites foaled in January, 26 of them won and the profit level was understandably large (48p per £1 staked). Conversely, a profit of 20p per £1 risked was generated by laying those beasts foaled in April and May. No such advantage accrued later in the season when presumably the late foals had "caught up".

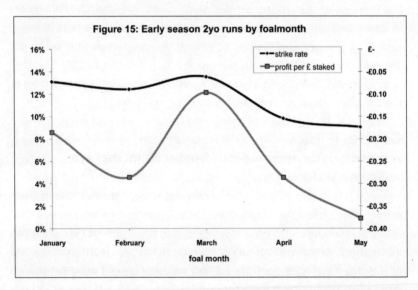

Figure 15: Early season 2yo runs by foalmonth

Trip

Is it possible to make money backing horses stepping up or down in trip? (Flat)

This is one of those variables about which much is spoken but little is actually known. "Should appreciate the step up in trip" we so often hear, or "shaped like he needed the extra furlong". My view is that the majority of these statements are unthinking. I often check the comment, then view the race online to be left thinking "he didn't need a longer trip, just a much weaker race!" The key to analysing steps up and down in trip is to look at each race distance on an individual basis. For example, trends that apply to a mile don't seem to apply to 12 furlongs. The clearest patterns pertain to the longer distances, which are specialisms. Take the distance of 1m6f as an example, I found 198 beasts stepping up to this trip (by at least 2f) and they returned a profit of 12p (per £1 staked). But that's not the interesting part. There was an interaction effect with age whereby the three-year-olds in the sample showed a huge loss, the four-year-olds broke even, but those over four years of age were handsomely in profit (50p per £1 staked) – that's what I call a "meaningful" trend. Incidentally, fancied horses did poorly as well, the profits seemed clustered in my favoured 4/1 – 8/1 band. Accordingly, many horses thought to "need" the longer trip must have failed.

Course

Is it possible to make a profit from runners that are switching surfaces?

Yes, in a big way. There is little to be said about horses moving from artificial surfaces (previous race) to turf (current race), except that odds-on favourites do return a slight profit. Things get much more interesting when we consider horses switching from turf to the all-weather surfaces though. Laying odds-on qualifiers results in a whopping profit. In fact, if you had laid the 242 such runners in my sample to £100 backers' stakes each time, then a payout of £3,300 would have been the reward. In terms of laying odds-on favourites, that sort of return is legendary. Notably, if we split that sample up again into fibresand or polytrack, a strong trend emerges. All of the profit comes from the polytrack part of the sample. In fact, if we **back** the runners moving from turf to fibresand (under 2/1) we make a respectable profit of 12p per pound staked. Runners moving between the two artificial surfaces performed poorly, especially in the case of those transferring from polytrack to fibresand. There were only 40 qualifiers but 24 of them lost resulting in an eye-popping profit of 37p per pound risked, which is massive in the context of laying odds-on shots; an example of a meaningful trend.

Does it pay to back course and distance winners? (Flat)

This is a variable which is very prominent, appearing as it does in black type every time we open a racing paper. It seems to shout: "I've already done exactly what is being asked of me, so back me!" It should therefore come as no surprise that these runners do well but are not profitable to back (losing around 24p per £1 staked). So I examined the fate of top-rated runners. In this case, C and D winners were still losers on the book, but course winners returned a good profit of 27p per £1 staked. I found 343 and backing them each to the tune of £100 would have netted us around £9,300.

Is there any profit in trainer-track trends? (Jumps)

I don't approve of endlessly protracted analyses concerning each handler's runners at individual tracks, broken down into categories. Nevertheless, the concept underlying the backing of a trainer's runners at a specific track is sound, so I looked to shore up this method by increasing the sample size. I selected *every* runner the trainer had at each track and it became clear at which tracks the leading handlers had the most success. To take this analysis a step further, I looked at the results season by season and tried to assess whether they had been caused by an underlying trend or merely a handful of results. Almost all of the profitable trends involved trainers sending runners to favoured local tracks. So in a roundabout way, we get a possible answer to the traveller's check question, which asks whether horses making big journeys are worth following. A typical example of the trends I found is the performance of Jonjo O'Neill's runners at one of his local tracks, Worcester. Of the 133 I found, approximately a quarter won returning a profit of £3,200 to £100 stakes. Most notably, the profit proved to be highly consistent over time. Other good examples include Nigel Twiston-Davies' runners at Warwick and Cheltenham, although the latter was partially spoilt by a poor festival in 2011.

The Twister" – Nigel Twiston-Davies with his son Sam at Cheltenham after Sam had won the Paddy Power Gold Cup on Little Josh

Class

Does form stand up better in classier races? (Flat)

Yes it does. Although favourites actually do better in the lower echelons (almost breaking even below Class 4), top-rated runners *excel* in racing's top-draw events. This is a "mighty oak" trend which never seems to change. I found 787 top-rated runners in Class 1 stakes races. Nearly 30 per cent of them won yielding a profit of £15,400 to our customary £100 wagers. Clearly, form works out very well in the ordered world of Class 1 events, not least because of the high prize money and the (near) absence of non-trying. Notably, top-weights in the better handicaps (above 90) come very close to breaking even.

Is it more profitable to back horses stepping up or down in class? (Flat)

This variable isn't as important as many people think. There are circumstances in which a small profit can be made by laying horses that are stepping up in class. The tried and tested way of assessing "class" is prize money. Looking at favourites only, I split my sample up into bands according to the difference in prize money between the present race and the previous one. There was a modest but highly reliable profit to be made from laying horses that were contesting races in which the first prize was at least £5,000 more than in the previous race.

Whereas favourites make great fodder for laying systems, top-rated runners flick the switches when it comes to backing. So I looked at the performance of top-rated animals in the same manner. We already know that top-rated horses perform exceptionally well in Class 1 events so this is where I focussed my efforts. Put simply, there is money to be made by backing these runners when they are stepping up or down in class by £20,000 or more (first prize). The return on investment was a very pleasing 42p per £1 staked (239 qualifiers). To complete the picture, I want to introduce a variable I use to good effect. It's the difference between the first prize in the present race and the *actual* amount won by the horse on its last outing. This accounts for the fact that a horse may have *contested* a good race last time out, but failed to win any money. Even if we consider *all* runners, there are tidy profits to be made by focussing on animals running in races that have a first prize which is at least £5,000 below the amount *actually won* last time.

How easy is it to make money using class pars? (Flat)

Very easy. I was able to cobble something good together at the first attempt. I chose to look at Group 1 races with a first prize of between £100k and £150k. This narrow band was used because the whole point of class figures is that you are assessing the standard which is needed to win a race of a specific class, and simply saying "Group 1" races is imprecise. I limited the sample to three-year-old plus races as I felt the maturation of juveniles would muddy the waters somewhat; the better three-year-olds are very close to their elders in terms of speed when running in the classier races. To develop the class figures I used the *Raceform* "split second" speed ratings gained over the previous three outings and took the best figure. What I found was that the speed rating needed to win these races was around the 111-112 mark. In my sample, there were 61 runners whose best speed rating was 110 or less, they all lost bar one (81p lost per £1 staked). Of those rated 111 and above according to my technique, there were 65 of which 14 won (21.5 per cent SR), thus returning a profit of £2,600 to £100 stakes (40p per £1 staked). Enough said!

Can you profit from trends relating to the owner?

That's a big yes. While the trainer is often the focal point for theories about how a horse is placed, the owner has a strong hand, particularly an influential owner with a large string of runners in his colours. These guys make a huge difference to a stable's bottom line and they can pull some strings. The simplest way to exploit the trends is to realise that owners often like to see their horses win in person – which is, after all, the whole raison d'etre of owning a racehorse. For this reason it's worth gleaning whether an owner frequents or favours a certain racecourse. Sometimes it's possible to piece together what is going on behind closed doors. For instance, an owner with a big string may not have many runners for a good while and then the switch gets flicked and they start popping up and winning all over the place. In this scenario, one intuits that there were some "words" exchanged between owner and trainer. A fellow with a large string of horses on the flat is the hotel magnate Dr Marwan Koukash, who counts Liverpool as his adopted home. Clearly, Dr Koukash enjoys seeing his horses win close to home. His colours popped up a lot at Haydock and Chester in 2010, with his runners seeming to fare much better at the latter venue. Indeed, they ran well enough to merit closer attention in 2011. Sure enough, his 2011 strike rate at the Cheshire course (so far) has been over 21% with a profit level of 32p per £1 staked. Incidentally, every one of his 32 runners at Haydock has been beaten.

Follow Dr Marwan Koukash at Chester

Is there more value to be had betting in the "getting out stakes"? (Flat)

No! I tried various approaches to see if the last race of the day showed unique betting patterns but none were forthcoming. I guess you can't win a coconut every time.

Weighing In

So, what to make of all the stats and trends? I am not suggesting that anyone simply operate all the systems I have written about, even though this would probably generate a respectable profit for a while. It's the principles underlying the systems that matter; the train of thought that leads one to alter and refine an approach until the profit has been tapped into. This endeavour is characterised by many dead ends and failures, but also by flashes of insight and leaps of critical thinking. We are drawn to ask questions like: "this may not work but have I selected the right variable or treated the data in the right way?" At heart, it is an inquisitive process illuminated by a healthy scepticism towards the conventional wisdom of the betting crowd.

In order to oppose the views of others, you have to understand them, or as Michael Corleone said in *The Godfather* **"one thing I learned from Pop was to try and think as people around you think"**. An apt quotation, bearing in mind quite a few professional punters seem to have experience of organised crime, albeit sometimes from being at the wrong end of it! There is a sort of strange affinity between gamblers and gangsters. Several prohibition-era mafiosi tried to beat the rap for tax evasion by claiming that their earnings came from the racetrack.

In Part 3, I considered many variables that we might focus on when preparing to bet. We cannot take them all into account, so which ones hold sway? Although there is no hard and fast answer to that, the analyses in Part 3 provide a model of how we can make that choice. So we have reached the last of my seven fundamental betting truths: **the art of betting is to fathom which particular variables hold the key to each unique race.**

I was told a story the other day which demonstrates this principle very well. An emergency plumbing expert was called to a large factory overnight, in which the basement had rapidly begun to flood. He guaranteed he could solve the problem but said that his fee would be £10,020. Because of the risk the flooding posed to the machinery, the manager on site agreed to the plumber's terms. When he arrived, he was faced with hundreds of valves, pipes, and gauges. Yet, he located the problem straight away and sealed off a pipe with one flick of his wrench. It had taken him under two minutes to avert the impending crisis. Indignant, the site manager queried "it cost us £10,020 for you to stop that valve?"

"No", explained the expert plumber, "it cost you £20 for me to stop the valve, and £10,000 for knowing which one to stop." That is the expertise of a successful bettor in a nutshell. It is also the reason why, at present, the human brain generally trumps the computer's processor when it comes to making money from betting. The computer essentially applies the same model to every race whereas the expert can employ a different approach every time.

Our research is also about understanding numbers, and the true meaning of the trends that lie within them. In essence, this means judging what our results signify and how likely it is that they will be repeated in a new sample. We are compelled to fight a powerful delusion which leads us to falsely infer the existence of patterns and then justify them with plausible-sounding narratives. This is why we have to remain open to the idea that racing data are full of apparent trends which have no underlying cause and cannot therefore be harnessed for our gain. To return to our mining analogy, these false patterns might be likened to the iron pyrite which so dazzled the early prospectors: **fool's gold**.

The means of actually carrying out research are of far less importance than the mindset underlying the whole enterprise. Nevertheless, I need to broach this topic. When I started writing books about betting a decade ago, the facility to analyse vast sets of racing data put me in a privileged position. Back then data was far harder to come by then, there were few bespoke software solutions for analysing it, hardware for the home computing market could barely handle the task, and the functionality of the internet was a shadow of what it is today. Yet as I write this in 2011, everything has changed: racing databases are easy to acquire and inexpensive, there are software- and web-based solutions that can query these databases rapidly, and very modest home computers can handle the task with consummate ease.

While the commercially available database options, some of which are listed in the resources guide at the back of this book, are satisfactory, to have complete control you need to manipulate the data directly. This allows you to go beyond the structures imposed by formbook software and answer pretty much any question that you can conceive of. Also, if you are using a method that is unique to you then there is a much greater chance you will develop an edge over gamblers who are, in effect, all working with the same tools. Some of the potent trends I have reported in this book would not have been easy to research using formbook software or a web-based service. To manipulate the data, you need to write programmes – which are in themselves simply lists of instructions. So it follows that, before you contemplate the specifics of any programming languages, you would need the ability to conceive of the operations you wish to perform *in plain English!*

Programming instructions merely describe the process you would follow with the data manually if you had the time and motivation to analyse it cell by cell. But this constitutes a great deal of time and motivation. During the preparation of this book, I became a little frustrated with the speed of a programme I had written, its purpose being to provide performance ratings for each runner based on its previous six runs. There were 835,267 runners in the dataset. I looked at the code to see how I could make it more efficient – the first thing that I noticed was that it performed 73 billion calculations in total. According to a conservative estimate, these would have taken me 105,000 working years to complete manually, by which time – so a boffin I know tells me – all life on earth would have been swallowed up by a new ice age. Hence the value of automation!

I use perhaps the easiest method going which is to write code in Visual Basic for Excel which operates on racing data that I keep in Microsoft Excel spreadsheets. When I started analysing data in this way, I learnt the few scraps of programming language I would need by trial and error over a few days. Since that time, I have refined my knowledge and found neater and more elegant ways to do the same thing slightly better. Nevertheless, my programming skills and ability are *extremely* limited. I would go as far as to say that, if you are able to understand this book, then you are certainly capable of programming your own code to test racing systems. In truth, the major drawback to programming is that it is very time-consuming, even if you know *exactly* what you are doing. The specifics of programming are undoubtedly beyond the ken of this book, but I wanted to broach the subject anyway, as it helps me to suggest an answer to the question of what you might do with the information I have presented. Even without learning how to programme, you can still exert complete control over your research: there are various web-based services that introduce you to programmers who are willing to work on ad-hoc projects for remarkably small fees.

The decision tree is as follows:

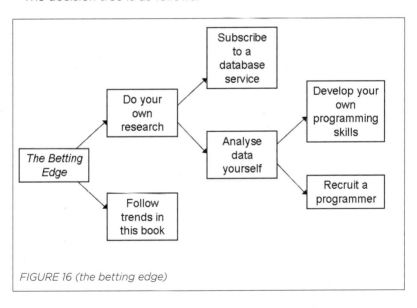

FIGURE 16 (the betting edge)

I will leave you with my seven fundamental truths of betting, there are probably others, but these represent a good starting point:

1) The betting market is a bucket of crabs
2) Profit is a fragile and transient creature and its most fearsome predators are publicity and time itself
3) The pattern of results in racing is a *chaotic* process
4) We are concerned directly with the betting market, but only *indirectly* with the performance of horses
5) We can only win if we take a *long-term* view
6) There is a *band* of prices which is favourable to us when backing
7) The secret of betting is knowing *which* variables to focus on in each race

Glossary

Alan Potts: A professional backer, author, and racehorse owner.

Apprentice: An inexperienced Flat jockey, benefiting from an allowance.

Barney Curley: An Irish trainer who has enjoyed careers as a gambler, bookmaker, charity organiser and even a pop group manager. He is known for his forthright views and involvement in legendary gambling coups. You can read about them in *Giving A Little Back* (Collins Wilkie, 1999).

Backer: One who backs (places a bet on) a horse.

Betting exchange: Betting exchanges usurp the traditional role of the bookmaker by serving as intermediaries that allow bettors with opposing viewpoints to effectively bet against each other. Although betting exchanges typically operate through the medium of the internet, it is possible to place such bets by telephone also.

Black swan event: According to Nassim Nicholas Taleb's definition, a black swan is a large-impact, hard-to-predict, and rare event beyond the realm of normal expectations. The term *black swan* comes from the ancient Western conception that "all swans are white".

Breeders' Cup: A prestigious American race meeting held in late autumn. The fixture comprises championship flat races on dirt (the typical racing surface used in America) and on turf. More than any other meeting, the Breeders' Cup attracts challengers from around the globe including a notable European contingent.

Cesarewitch: A long-distance handicap traditionally held on Newmarket's Rowley Mile course in the late autumn of each year. Runners drawn high or low have an appalling record whereas those drawn in the middle stalls are far more likely to win. The reason for this bias might be the width of the track at Newmarket and the corresponding necessity of being "covered-up".

Chalk: In days long gone, the favourite became known as the "chalk" because the horse's name would disappear in chalk dust as the bookie constantly erased and altered the horse's odds.

Claimer: An apprentice or conditional jockey who is claiming a weight advantage carries 3lbs, 5lbs, or 7lbs less in weight than it would otherwise have done.

Classic: The five Classics are the principal flat races of each season contested by three-year-old runners only. The 1000 guineas (fillies) and 2000 guineas (colts) are run over a mile at Newmarket (Rowley) in early May. The Oaks (fillies) and Derby (colts – also open to fillies) are contested over 1m 4f at Epsom in early June, and the St. Leger (fillies and colts) is run over 1m 6f 132y at Doncaster in mid September.

Collateral form: If two horses have never raced against each other but have both raced against a third animal then one can use this "collateral" form to infer how the two runners in question would fare against each other.

Colt: A colt is a male horse under the age of five that has not yet been castrated. Conversely, a filly is a female horse under the age of five, at which point she is designated a mare.

Conditional rider: Conditionals are the National Hunt equivalent of the apprentice jockeys who ride on the flat.

Connections: The connections of a horse are those who have a shared interest in the animal, principally the owner(s), but to a less extent any person who is "connected" with the horse in some way, e.g., the trainer, the head lad from the stable, etc. There is a discussion of the term "connections" on page 76 of *The Racing Tribe* (1999, Metro).

David Ashforth: A racing journalist and backer who wrote a highly respected and forthright Saturday column for the *Racing Post* and has authored an excellent and very funny gambling autobiography *Hitting the Turf* (1995, Headline). David stepped down from the *Racing Post* at the end of 2010.

Downgrade: A horse "on the downgrade" is suffering a decline in performance.

Draw: A horse's allotted position in the starting stalls that are used in flat races.

Dutching: Sharing the risk of losing across a number or runners by backing more than one selection in a race or event. The process calculates the correct stake to place on each selection so that the return is the same if any of them wins.

Ebor handicap and the draw bias: Refer to page 56 of *Against the Crowd* (1995, Aesculus Press).

Form: When displayed in a newspaper, form (the record of previous performances) is often abbreviated into a series of numbers or characters, each representing a race. The races are listed in chronological order with the most recent race appearing on the far right of the list. The numbers represent the finishing position of the horse (e.g., 1 = finished 1st, 0 = finished 10th or worse). Alphabetic characters generally indicate a failure to complete the race (e.g., F = horse fell, P = horse was pulled-up).

Gaff track: The smaller, more provincial racecourses are commonly referred to as the "gaff" tracks.

Gelding: A horse that has been gelded (castrated).

Get on: To "get on" is to successfully place a bet, i.e., to have it accepted.

The Guineas: *See* 'Classic'.

Jocking-off: When a jockey is replaced for a given ride (normally by a senior rider).

Kickback: The dirt, sand, or turf kicked back by the hooves of horses. Kickback impairs the vision of the horses behind.

Lay: To "lay" a horse is to accept another's bet and therefore act in the role that is traditionally associated with the bookmaker. Hence, if you accept a bet of £10 on a horse whose odds stand at 10/1 then you will win the £10 stake should the horse lose but you

will be liable to pay the £100 winnings to the other bettor if the horse does indeed win. To lay a horse is the opposite of backing it, which is to bet that the horse will win.

Lay-off: In order to reduce his liabilities, a bookmaker may elect to "lay-off" part of a bet he has accepted by backing the same horse to win with another bookmaker. If the bookmaker manages to achieve the ideal of backing the horse in question at higher odds than those he offered himself then he is said to have "got on velvet" because profit is ensured.

Layer: Bookmakers are sometimes referred to as layers.

Liquidity: A term, often applied to the exchange markets, that describes the amount of money that is 'flowing' through the market at a given time. If liquidity is high then it's easy to be matched and there is plenty of trading activity which gives the prices mobility. A static market with low liquidity is less likely to be a true reflection of the various runners' probabilities of success.

Mudlark: A horse that is thought to prefer very soft ground.

Nap: A nap is one's principal selection. The word originates from the parlance of card games and is an abbreviation of Napoleon.

Naps table: The profit derived from backing the naps put forward by various newspaper tipsters is displayed in a table that can be found in the *Racing Post*.

Novice: Once a horse has recorded its first victory, it will relinquish its novice status from the beginning of the following season onwards. In 2008, the BHA remodelled the structure of novice chases by introducing the following categories: beginner's chases for horses who have not won over fences, novice handicaps, and WFA novice chases.

Nursery: A handicap for two-year-old horses.

Penalties: Various weight penalties are applied to runners; predominantly those taking part in stakes races. More information appears on the BHA's website: http://rules.britishhorseracing. com/Orders-and-rules&staticID=126775

Dr. Peter May: A writer on the subject of selection methods who has penned nine books including *Forecasting Methods for Horse Racing* (1998, Raceform).

Phil Bull: The enigmatic Phil Bull was a professional gambler of note who made his fortune largely by devising a method of producing ratings based on race times. Based on this principle, he sired the *Timeform* organisation, which is now owned by *Betfair*.

Projected starting prices: The estimated starting prices which are printed in the racing press.

Rag: Rank outsider with no realistic chance of winning.

SP (over-round) percentages: There is a margin built into the bookmakers' prices, which is the mechanism that enables them to generate a profit in the long-term. If one placed bets on every runner in a race so as to return £100 whichever horse won, the sum of the stakes would normally exceed the £100 expected winnings. When this occurs, a book is said to be over-round. The over-round percentage is a statistic that describes the extent of the bookmakers' margin. If one needed to stake £110 to win a certain £100 by spreading one's stakes in the manner described above, then the percentage would be 110 per cent. When this percentage is below 100, it is possible to make a certain profit by backing every runner in the book. In these rare cases the book is considered under-round. The over-round book would ensure bookmakers a long-term profit on its own if backers were to bet randomly. However, backers demonstrate a marked preference for the horses which are generally considered to have a greater chance of winning.

Steeplechase: Steeplechases are commonly referred to as chases and horses that compete in these races are known as "chasers". The steeplechase draws its lineage from cross-country events that were staged between the church steeples of neighbouring towns.

Tattersalls: The mid-priced Tattersalls enclosure is typically situated between the members' enclosure (the most expensive) and the silver ring (least expensive). The name is taken from Richard Tattersall, who founded the world's first bloodstock auction house in 1766.

Tissue: The compilation of odds drawn up by industry representatives, upon which the on-course bookmakers base their initial prices.

Tote: An abbreviation of 'the horserace totalisator board'; a pool-based betting system that was introduced to British racecourses in 1929. Part of the profit that the Tote produces is used to support racing.

Tote deductions for "win" bets: If you spread a stake of £115.61 between all the runners in a given race and yours were the only bets then the "win" pool would equal £100 after a 13.5 per cent deduction.

Trouble the judge: The judge is a racecourse official who determines the finishing order of the runners and the distances that separate them. If a horse is involved in the competition for the higher places then the animal is said to have "troubled the judge".

Unexposed: The ability of horses with little public form (i.e., in races) cannot easily be assessed in comparison with their rivals. Such runners are said to be "unexposed".

Upgrade: A horse "on the upgrade" is an improving animal.

Weak market: When there is very little betting activity, a market is said to be "weak". In such markets, prices are relatively static as there is little betting interest in the race.

Yard: A racing stable is commonly referred to as a "yard".

Resources

Here is a selection of links that may be of use. I hope that they're all still active by the time this book goes to press.

General ("search" on each site for what you want to view)
Video: youtube.com *Try "channel four racing funny" for example*
Online encyclopaedia: wikipedia.com *Try "Barney Curley" for example*

Forums and blogs:
forum.punterslounge.com
uk-betting-tips.co.uk
horseracingsystemsuk.com
horse-betting-systems.co.uk
flatstats.co.uk
theracingforum.co.uk/horse-racing-forum
betting.betfair.com/horse-racing
sportismadeforbetting.com
bettingmarket.com

Betting:
Free bets: freebets.co.uk
Odds checker: oddschecker.com

Jobs:
betrecruit.com
bettingjobs.com/
jobs.careersinracing.com/
hyperiongaming.com/

Racing statistics, ratings, articles and systems:
ukhorseracing.co.uk/reviews/smartsig.asp (highly recommended)
racingresearch.co.uk
timeform.com
raceform.co.uk
proformracing.co.uk
horseracebase.com
adrianmassey.no-ip.org/web1/
pjmr.freeserve.co.uk
infineform.com
informracing.com
flatstats.co.uk

formbet.co.uk

Information:
sportinglife.com
racingpost.com

Books and form:
racingpost.com/shop

Links:
ukhorseracing.co.uk/links

Horse racing administration and industry:
BHA: britishhorseracing.com
BHA rules site: rules.britishhorseracing.com
British Racing School: brs.org.uk/Home
Northern Racing College: northernracingcollege.co.uk
British Racecourses: britishracecourses.org
Weatherbys (administers racing): weatherbys.co.uk
The Jockey Club: thejockeyclub.co.uk

Weather:
metoffice.gov.uk
accuweather.com
bbc.co.uk/weather
positiveweathersolutions.co.uk (long-term weather)

Computer programming (books):
Excel VBA Programming for Dummies by John Walkenbach
Writing Excel Macros with VBA by Steven Roman

Other:
Horse welfare: animalaid.org.uk/images/pdf/unsporting.pdf
A good jargon buster: newmarketracecourses.co.uk/racing/new-to-racing/jargon-buster/

APPENDICES

Weight for Age Tables and Racecourse Characteristics

TABLE 10: WEIGHT-FOR-AGE SCALE (NORTHERN-HEMISPHERE BRED, FLAT HORSES)

(Distance) (furlongs)	2yos				3yos														4yos									
	5	6	7	8	5	6	7	8	9	10	11	12	13	14	15	16	18	20	9	10	11	12	13	14	15	16	18	20
Jan 1-15	-	-	-	-	15	16	18	20	22	23	24	25	26	27	28	29	31	33	1	2	3	4	5	6	6	7	8	9
Jan 16-31	-	-	-	-	15	16	18	20	22	23	24	25	26	27	28	29	31	33	1	2	3	4	5	6	6	7	8	9
Feb 1-14	-	-	-	-	13	14	16	18	21	22	23	24	25	26	27	28	30	32	-	1	2	3	4	5	5	6	7	8
Feb 15-28	-	-	-	-	12	13	15	17	21	22	23	24	25	26	27	28	30	32	-	1	2	3	4	5	5	6	7	8
Mar 1-15	47	-	-	-	13	14	16	18	20	21	22	23	24	25	26	27	29	31	-	-	1	2	3	4	4	5	6	7
Mar 16-31	44	-	-	-	12	13	15	17	19	20	21	22	23	24	25	26	28	30	-	-	1	2	3	4	4	5	6	7
Apr 1-15	41	-	-	-	11	12	14	15	17	19	20	21	22	23	24	25	27	29	-	-	-	1	2	3	3	4	5	6
Apr 15-30	38	44	-	-	10	11	13	14	15	17	19	20	21	22	23	24	26	28	-	-	-	1	1	2	3	4	5	6
May 1-15	36	41	-	-	9	10	12	13	14	15	17	19	20	21	22	23	25	27	-	-	-	-	-	1	2	3	4	5
May 16-31	34	38	-	-	7	9	11	12	13	14	15	17	19	20	21	22	24	26	-	-	-	-	-	-	1	2	3	4
Jun 1-15	32	36	-	-	6	8	10	11	12	13	14	15	17	19	20	21	23	25	-	-	-	-	-	-	-	1	2	3
Jun 16-30	30	33	38	-	6	7	9	10	11	12	13	14	15	17	19	20	22	24	-	-	-	-	-	-	-	-	1	2
Jul 1-15	28	31	35	-	5	6	8	9	10	11	12	13	14	15	17	19	21	23	-	-	-	-	-	-	-	-	-	1
Jul 16-31	26	28	32	37	4	5	7	8	9	10	11	12	13	14	15	17	20	22	-	-	-	-	-	-	-	-	-	-
Aug 1-15	24	26	30	34	3	4	6	7	8	9	10	11	12	13	14	15	18	20	-	-	-	-	-	-	-	-	-	-
Aug 16-31	22	24	27	31	2	3	5	6	7	8	9	10	11	12	13	14	16	18	-	-	-	-	-	-	-	-	-	-
Sep 1-15	20	22	25	28	1	2	4	5	6	7	8	9	10	11	12	13	14	16	-	-	-	-	-	-	-	-	-	-
Sep 16-30	19	21	23	26	1	2	3	4	5	6	7	8	9	10	11	12	13	14	-	-	-	-	-	-	-	-	-	-
Oct 1-15	18	20	22	24	-	1	2	3	4	5	6	7	8	9	10	11	12	13	-	-	-	-	-	-	-	-	-	-
Oct 16-31	-	-	-	-	-	1	2	3	4	5	6	7	8	9	10	11	12	12	-	-	-	-	-	-	-	-	-	-

Distance (furlongs)	2yos				3yos														4yos									
	5	6	7	8	5	6	7	8	9	10	11	12	13	14	15	16	18	20	9	10	11	12	13	14	15	16	18	20
Nov 1-15	17	19	21	23	-	-	1	2	3	4	5	6	7	8	8	9	10	11	-	-	-	-	-	-	-	-	-	-
Nov 16-30	17	18	20	22	-	-	1	2	3	4	5	6	7	8	8	9	10	11	-	-	-	-	-	-	-	-	-	-
Dec 1-15	16	17	19	21	-	-	-	1	2	3	4	5	6	7	7	8	9	10	-	-	-	-	-	-	-	-	-	-
Dec 16-31	16	17	19	20	-	-	-	1	2	3	4	5	6	7	7	8	9	10	-	-	-	-	-	-	-	-	-	-

TABLE 11: WEIGHT-FOR-AGE SCALE (NORTHERN-HEMISPHERE BRED, JUMPS HORSES)

| Distance (furlongs) | Hurdles and NHF | | | | | | Steeplechases | | | | | |
| | 3yos | | | 4yos | | | 4yos | | | 5yos | | |
	2m	2½m	3m	2m	2½m	3m	2m	2½m	3m	2m	2½m	3m
Jan 1-15	-	-	-	12	13	14	-	-	-	4	5	6
Jan 16-31	-	-	-	11	12	13	-	-	-	3	4	5
Feb 1-14	-	-	-	10	11	12	-	-	-	2	3	4
Feb 15-28	-	-	-	9	10	11	-	-	-	1	2	3
Mar 1-15	-	-	-	8	9	10	-	-	-	-	1	2
Mar 16-31	-	-	-	7	8	9	-	-	-	-	-	1
Apr 1-15	-	-	-	6	7	8	-	-	-	-	-	-
Apr 16-30	-	-	-	5	6	7	-	-	-	-	-	-
May 1-15	22	23	24	4	5	6	18	19	20	-	-	-
May 16-31	22	23	24	4	5	6	18	19	20	-	-	-
Jun 1-15	21	22	23	3	4	5	17	18	19	-	-	-
Jun 16-30	21	22	23	3	4	5	17	18	19	-	-	-
Jul 1-15	20	21	22	2	3	4	16	17	18	-	-	-
Jul 16-31	20	21	22	2	3	4	15	16	17	-	-	-
Aug 1-15	19	20	21	1	2	3	14	15	16	-	-	-
Aug 16-31	19	20	21	1	2	3	13	14	15	-	-	-
Sep 1-15	18	19	20	-	1	2	12	13	14	-	-	-
Sep 16-30	18	19	20	-	1	2	11	12	13	-	-	-
Oct 1-15	17	18	19	-	-	1	10	11	12	-	-	-
Oct 16-31	17	18	19	-	-	1	9	10	11	-	-	-
Nov 1-15	16	17	18	-	-	-	8	9	10	-	-	-
Nov 16-30	15	16	17	-	-	-	7	8	9	-	-	-
Dec 1-15	14	15	16	-	-	-	6	7	8	-	-	-
Dec 16-31	13	14	15	-	-	-	5	6	7	-	-	-

TABLE 12. CHARACTERISTICS OF JUMPS RACECOURSES

Course	RH/LH	Flat/Undual	Sharp/Galloping	Run-In	Fences	Notes
Aintree (National)	LH	Flat	Galloping	2f		With sharp turns and big, steep fences
Aintree (Mildmay)	LH	Flat	Sharp	3f	Stiff	
Ascot	RH	Slightly Undulating	Galloping	240y	Stiff	Uphill finish
Ayr	LH	Flat	Galloping	210y		
Bangor-on-Dee	LH	Flat	Sharp	325y		Front runners
Carlisle	RH	Undulating	Long-striding	300y		
Cartmel	LH	Flat	Sharp	4f	Stiff but fair	
Catterick	LH	Undulating	Sharp	240y		Uphill finish
Cheltenham	LH	Undulating	Galloping	2f-4f	Stiff fences	
Chepstow	LH	Very Undulating	Long-striding	240y		Emphasis on stamina
Doncaster	LH	Flat	Galloping	1f		
Exeter	RH	Undulating	Somewhat sharp	300y		Uphill run in; emphasis on stamina
Fakenham	LH	Undulating	Sharp	1f		
Ffos Las	LH	Flat	Sharp	3.5f		
Folkestone	RH	Undulating	Very Sharp	230y	Easy	
Fontwell	F8	Flat	Somewhat sharp	230y		Specialist's course; hurdle = LH
Haydock	LH	Flat	Galloping	2f	Stiff	Hurdle track is sharp
Hereford	RH	Undulating	Galloping	300y	Somewhat stiff	Easy turns except last bend
Hexham	LH	Undulating	Galloping	1f	Easy	Stiff uphill climb to finishing straight; stamina test when soft
Huntingdon	RH	Flat	Galloping	1f	Stiff	3 tricky fences for novices
Kelso	LH	Undulating	Sharp	2f		2 downhill fences, hurdles track very sharp

Course	RH/LH	Flat/Undual	Sharp/Galloping	Run-In	Fences	Notes
Leicester	RH	Undulating	Galloping	250y		Emphasis on stamina; last 3f uphill
Lingfield	LH	Undulating	Somewhat sharp	1f		Tight downhill turn into the straight
Ludlow	RH	Flat	Sharp	1f		Hurdle track not as sharp
Market Rasen	RH	Undulating	Sharp	250y		
Musselburgh	RH	Flat	Sharp	150y		
Newbury	LH	Flat	Galloping	250y	Stiff	
Newcastle	LH	Slightly Undulating	Galloping	220y	Somewhat stiff	Gradual rise in home straight
Newton Abbot	RH	Flat	Sharp	300y		
Perth	RH	Flat	Somewhat sharp	1.5f		Fairly easy turns
Plumpton	LH	Undulating	Sharp	200y		Uphill finish
Sandown	RH	Undulating	Handy	1f	Stiff	Stiff uphill climb to finish; three "railway" fences very close together
Sedgefield	LH	Undulating	Sharp	200y		
Southwell	LH	Flat	Sharp	1f		
Stratford	LH	Flat	Sharp	1f		
Taunton	RH	Slightly Undulating	Sharp	150y		Climb to finish
Towcester	LH	Undulating	Galloping	1f		Uphill run-in; emphasis on stamina
Uttoxeter	LH	Flat	Galloping	180y	Fair	East bends
Warwick	LH	Undulating	Sharp	2f		Succession of five fences in back straight
Wetherby	LH	Flat	Galloping	200y		
Wincanton	RH	Slightly Undulating	Galloping	200y		
Wolverhampton	LH	Flat	Sharp	200y		
Worcester	LH	Flat	Galloping	5f		

Note: Run-in refers to the length of the finishing straight

TABLE 13. CHARACTERISTICS OF FLAT RACECOURSES

Course	RH/LH	Flat/Undulating	Sharp/Galloping	Run-In	Notes
Ascot	RH	Slightly Undulating	Galloping	2.5f	
Ayr	LH	Slightly Undulating	Galloping	4f	Easy turns
Bath	LH	Slightly Undulating	Galloping	4f	Stiff finish; kink to the left two furlongs prior to finish
Beverley	RH	Slightly Undulating	Mostly galloping	2.5f	Uphill run in; worth opposing doubtful stayers
Brighton	LH	Very Undulating	Sharp	3.5f	Switchback, Specialist's Course- consider Epsom, Lingfield, and Bath form
Carlisle	RH	Undulating	Galloping	3.5f	Very steep finish
Catterick	LH	Undulating	Sharp	3f	
Chepstow	LH	Very Undulating	Long-striding	240y	Easy turns, requires much stamina if soft
Chester	LH	Flat	Very Sharp	230y	Need early speed; course specialists prevail
Doncaster	LH	Flat	Galloping	8f	Easy turns
Epsom	LH	Undulating	Somewhat sharp	4f	Downhill 5f. Easy turns bar Tattenham corner
Ffos Las	LH	Flat	Sharp	3.5f	
Folkestone	RH	Undulating	Very Sharp	2.5f	
Goodwood	RH	Very Undulating	Sharp	5f+	Fast start needed in sprints, needs nimble horses and course specialists
Hamilton	RH	Undulating	Sharp	5.5f	Uphill run in, ground can be very heavy in wet weather and stamina needed
Haydock	LH	Flat	Galloping	5f	Wide turns
Kempton	RH	Flat	Somewhat sharp	3.5f	Sharp bend into straight
Leicester	RH	Undulating	Galloping	5f	Last 3f all uphill, wide turns, testing stamina
Lingfield	LH	Undulating	Sharp	1f	Similar camber to Epsom, slight downhill into straight
Musselburgh	RH	Flat	Sharp	4f	
Newbury	LH	Flat	Galloping	4f	Good stamina test; very fair

Course	RH/LH	Flat/Undulating	Sharp/Galloping	Run-In	Notes
Newcastle	LH	Slightly Undulating	Galloping	4f	Steady uphill finish; easy turns, can become testing
Newmarket	RH	Slightly Undulating	Galloping	12f+	Very open, experience needed. There is a dip with an uphill finish
Newmarket (J)	RH	Slightly Undulating	Galloping	8f+	Steep finish
Nottingham	LH	Flat	Galloping	5f	Easy bends
Pontefract	LH	Undulating	Sharp	3f	Stiff final 2f
Redcar	LH	Flat	Galloping	5f	
Ripon	RH	Undulating	Sharp	5f	Gradual rising finish
Salisbury	RH	Flat	Galloping	4f	Final half mile uphill
Sandown	RH	Undulating	Galloping	3.5f	Uphill run-in
Southwell	LH	Flat	Sharp	3f	
Thirsk	LH	Undulating	Sharp	3.5f	
Warwick	LH	Undulating	Sharp	2f	
Windsor	F8	Flat	Sharp	5f	
Wolverhampton	LH	Flat	Sharp	380y	
Yarmouth	LH	Flat	Galloping	5f	Tight turns
York	LH	Flat	Galloping	6f	Wide turns, testing if soft

Note: Run-in refers to the length of the finishing straight

INDEX